# Casseroles & Stews

**DAVID & CHARLES**

Newton Abbot  London

**British Library Cataloguing in Publication Data**
Casseroles and stews.—(David & Charles Kitchen Workshop)
  1. Casserole cookery
  I. Gryteretter. *English*
  641.8′21    TX693

  ISBN 0-7153-8461-9

© Illustrations: A/S Hjemmet 1979
  Text: David & Charles 1983

Typeset by MS Filmsetting Ltd, Frome, Somerset
and printed in The Netherlands
by Smeets Offset BV, Weert
for David & Charles (Publishers) Limited
Brunel House, Newton Abbot, Devon

# Casseroles and Stews

*Casseroles and stews are perennially popular, both for everyday, and for parties, particularly in the colder months of the year. Their main advantages are:*

● Casseroles and stews can be prepared well in advance and re-heated before serving.
● Most casseroles and stews can be frozen very successfully.
● You can choose casserole ingredients and garnishes depending on taste, occasion and the state of your finances.
● Casseroles and stews can be economical, in that cheaper cuts which require longer cooking can be used.

Most casseroles and stews take a long time to cook but they more or less look after themselves after the initial preparation. They are ideal party food for busy people, as they can be prepared in advance, leaving plenty of time to clear up, lay the table, get ready – and even have a drink – before the guests arrive.

Most of the recipes will serve 6–8 people. Although our recipes are usually designed for the 'average' family consisting of 3–4 people, you might as well cook a larger amount at one time, and save or freeze some. Large casseroles take no longer, basically, to cook than small ones, so it would seem sensible to eat half and freeze the other half for later use. Set aside one day when you have plenty of time for a mass production of casseroles, and you will have something to serve for dinner that day and for family or emergency occasions in the future. You can also utilise the heat of the oven more economically, when cooking more than one dish in it.

**General Advice**
At the top of each recipe in this book you will find guidelines as to how to prepare the dish in question, but some more general advice is in order.
● When browning meat in casserole or frying pan, do not put too much in at one time. If you put too much meat in, the fat will cool and the meat will simmer instead of sauté and brown. You want the meat to sauté quickly to seal in all the goodness.

● Most casseroles and stews can be cooked in the oven at a temperature of about 180°C, 350°F, Gas 4, covered with a tight-fitting lid or doubled tinfoil. Make sure the liquid does not evaporate. You can prepare several dishes in the oven at the same time, providing they require the same temperature, which makes for economy.

● Obviously, the better the meat, the better your casserole should be, but in general, the meat used in casseroles is not from the most expensive cuts, but from those that require long, slow cooking to make them tender and to bring out their flavour. Cuts with a slight marbling of fat are excellent stewed or braised.

● The best casseroles, stews and braises require a good stock, preferably made at home from raw bones and vegetables. It is always a good idea to get some bones from the butcher when buying your meat – or indeed buy the meat *on* the bone and cook it initially *on* the bone. Never leave fish trimmings at the fishmonger, but use them to make the stock for your fish casserole.

● Always study the recipes carefully before you begin. Make sure you have all you need, both for the dish itself and for the garnishes, especially if you are going to eat it straightaway. If you are going to freeze the dish, or part of it, watch out for seasoning (see below), and make sure you have the proper freezer packaging materials.

● Many of the dishes contain several kinds of vegetables, herbs and spices. This does not mean you have to use them all. If one of the casserole recipes specifies both celeriac and parsnip, for instance, you can leave out one and use more of the other instead. The taste won't be quite the same, but near enough. You can also, for instance, substitute the meat specified in a recipe with leftover cooked meat, or indeed sausages, but a different cooking time will be required.

● Never be afraid to make changes to a recipe. Add a little more spice perhaps, or a vegetable you are particularly fond of. The real joy of cooking lies in experimenting, adding your own personal touch – although it must always be allied with common sense!

**Freezing**

Most casseroles and stews can be frozen. Some dishes, however, might contain some ingredient or a sauce, for instance, which could not happily be re-heated. We make this clear at the beginning of each recipe. Freeze casseroles and stews in tinfoil dishes with lids, ovenproof and freezerproof dishes or strong freezer bags. Stretch freezer bags over baking tins or rigid plastic containers, fill, and then put in freezer. When frozen, remove bags from containers, close securely, and replace in freezer. 'Squared' up this way, the casseroles will take up less room, making it easier to keep the freezer tidy. Remember to write date and contents clearly on the packages.

Do not over-season food you are going to freeze, as this reduces the time it will keep. It's best to *under-season* casseroles, as you can always season them at the last minute. Too much seasoning doesn't make frozen food inedible or a danger to health; but the fat in meat, fish and sauces or gravies has a greater tendency to go rancid if the frozen dish contains either salt, or if one or several of the ingredients are cured. As a general rule, unspiced or slightly spiced dishes will keep in the freezer for 4–6 months; dishes containing a lot of seasoning or cured meats will keep for 2–3 months only.

Many of the recipes specify fresh herbs and spices. These, too, should not be added to a dish to be frozen. Add when re-heated and ready for the table.

Thawing and re-heating of frozen casseroles and stews should be done in a thick bottomed pot or pan on low heat. If you have thickened the gravy in the dish, it is advisable to pour some water into the pan, so that the frozen food does not stick. If you have frozen the casserole in a tinfoil or ovenproof dish, you can re-heat in the oven at a temperature of 150–160°C, 300–325°F, Gas 3–4. Don't forget to remove lid from tinfoil dish (often made from cardboard), and re-cover with doubled tinfoil sheeting.

Handle ovenproof dishes with care: not all can be safely put directly into oven from freezer. When in doubt, leave the dish in the refrigerator for about 8 hr, or at room temperature for about 2–3 hr before putting into the oven.

# The Four Casseroles

*There are, basically, four main groups of casseroles.*

### Vegetable Casseroles
Nearly all vegetables are suitable for casseroling, accompanied by a couple of slices of bacon or meat juices. Filling ingredients like rice and pasta are often added. Vegetable casseroles do not take long to cook and are excellent everyday fare. They are also cheap to make, rich in vitamins and very tasty.

### Poultry Casseroles
These are also fairly economical, using fresh or frozen birds, pieces or boiling fowl. Chicken doesn't take long to cook, and as it is fairly bland, juicy and tasty vegetables and seasonings to accompany it can be infinitely varied.

### Fish Casseroles

These are not so common, but try some of our recipes and you will discover that both fish and shellfish make lovely casseroles. Vegetables, lemon, white wine, double cream and cheese add flavour to fish casseroles, which must always be seasoned with moderation.

### Meat Casseroles

The meat for braising and stewing can be the more economical cuts of beef, pork and lamb or mutton. The bones and fat indeed *add* flavour, but must always be removed before serving. Add vegetables and spices according to how much meat you have in your casserole. These casseroles take quite a long time to cook, so make a large quantity at a time.

# Herbs and Spices

Fresh herbs and spices add taste to every casserole. Always try to use fresh herbs, but both frozen and dried ones can be substituted – but remember that dried herbs generally have a stronger taste (so use *less* dried than fresh). In the following table you will find a list of herbs and spices, with suggestions as to how you can make the most of them, and how you yourself can cultivate them. There's a certain knack in seasoning correctly – not too much, not too little – but it can be acquired by always *tasting* what you are cooking. Our simple outline below is meant to be simply that, specifying which herbs and spices go best with the main casserole ingredient, but you can experiment. Don't use them all at the same time, though!

| INGREDIENT | HERBS AND SPICES |
|---|---|
| Fish | Curry powder, turmeric, saffron, caraway seeds, coriander, mixed spice or spice herbs, dill, bay leaves, parsley, lemon balm, chives, tarragon, chervil, fennel, marjoram |
| Pork | Curry powder, paprika, cayenne pepper, ginger, caraway seeds, bay leaves, parsley, rosemary, garlic, basil, fennel, tarragon |
| Beef | Paprika, cayenne pepper, nutmeg, mixed spice or allspice beans, bay leaf, garlic, rosemary, thyme, sage, marjoram, cress, horseradish |
| Veal | Curry powder, garlic, parsley, rosemary, dill, tarragon |
| Lamb and mutton | Curry powder, cayenne pepper, paprika, turmeric, dill, garlic, mint, marjoram, thyme, rosemary |
| Mince and sausage-meat dishes | Paprika, coriander, cayenne pepper, nutmeg, basil, marjoram, sage |
| Poultry | Paprika, curry powder, turmeric, cayenne pepper, tarragon, thyme, bay leaves, parsley, fennel, marjoram, sage, basil, lemon balm, garlic, horseradish |
| Game | Juniper berries, paprika, rosemary, thyme, bay leaves |
| Vegetables and salads | Nutmeg, paprika, curry powder, cayenne pepper, caraway seeds, parsley, chives, garlic, chervil, basil, marjoram. All herbs and spices are good in salads. |
| Egg dishes | Curry powder, paprika, cayenne pepper, nutmeg, parsley, chervil, dill, tarragon, basil, marjoram, garlic |
| Rice dishes, pizza and spaghetti | Thyme, caraway seeds, rosemary, ginger, parsley, chives, oregano, basil |
| Desserts | Cinnamon, cardamom, vanilla, ginger |
| Bread and Cakes | Caraway seeds, mixed spice or allspice beans, cloves, cinnamon, cardamom, vanilla, saffron, fennel, sesame seed |

**Bouquet Garni**
One of the commonest casserole ingredients is a bouquet garni, and there are many possible variations. Tie together with string, for instance, leek leaves, a sprig of parsley, a bay leaf, a celery leaf, and a sprig of thyme. If you leave a long end to the string, it can be tied to the pot handle, and suspended in the stew, thus making it easier to remove.

**Oregano**
Oregano belongs to the same family as marjoram, and is often substituted for sweet marjoram (it's often called pot marjoram). Use the leaves only, either fresh, dried or crushed. You can use it with fried fish, in mince and any dish with tomatoes. It is mostly used in pizzas and spaghetti dishes and also in chili con carne. It has a wonderfully warm, heady scent and flavour.

**Fennel**
There are two distinct varieties of fennel: the tall perennial herb that is cultivated for the fine flavour of its leaves, seeds and stems; and the smaller Florence fennel which is

# Herbs

*Cut fresh leaves, thin stems and new shoots off bought or home-grown herbs in season. Read a good herb gardening guide for more details about sowing, cultivating and harvesting. Pick leaves etc off plants before the first frosts, and wash thoroughly Freeze in portions (the best way) for a good supply through the winter. If you prefer to dry them, hang in small bunches in a dry and airy place. Dried herbs must be stored in tightly lidded dark glass jars. Remember that when dried, the herbs generally acquire a stronger taste, so use them sparingly.*

grown mainly for its swollen stem base and is used in salads and as a vegetable. Both varieties have a sweet, heady taste of aniseed.

Common or herb fennel grows well in a warm sunny position. Sow in March, April or May, and pick leaves from June onwards. Gather seeds in early autumn and dry. Dry or preferably freeze the frondy leaves of both common or Florence fennel.

The seeds are used sparingly with fish, pork, mushrooms and poultry, as well as in breads, soups and cakes. They can also be used to flavour pickling vinegars.

## Lemon Balm

The small dark green leaves of this plant, a hardy perennial, have a strong lemon scent when bruised. Fresh leaves can be used to flavour salads, soups, sauces and cold drinks. Dried leaves are used in, for instance, fruit salads, fruit soups, homemade wine, liqueurs and beer. Leaves can also be frozen.

## Sweet Marjoram

A half-hardy annual, low plant with grey-green, small hairy leaves and small pinky white flowers. Pot marjoram – oregano – is fully hardy, but tastes less sweet.

Marjoram grows in gardens, window boxes or flower pots, and grows best in full sun. Sow in March inside or under glass, and pick leaves and flowers in the summer.

The finely chopped leaves and flowers are used in all sorts of Italian dishes, often with basil. Marjoram can also be used in bouquets garnis, added to casseroles and soups, in tomato dishes, with pork, in dishes made from sausagemeat and also with blood sausages and liver pâté. Freeze for winter use or take cuttings in August and grow indoors.

## Garlic

Garlic can be grown from the cloves of a bulb bought from the greengrocer. It does best in a sunny position.

The green stems from a clove of garlic sown pointed end up in a pot on the window-sill all the year round can be chopped and added to salads or sprinkled over boiled potatoes, etc, to give a mild garlic flavour.

Crush garlic for casseroles etc, and if you want only a subtle taste of garlic,

rub the inside of the casserole or bowl with a split clove (particularly common with salads).

You can use garlic with almost everything, but in moderation, as its flavour is very strong. The juice of garlic is a very strong antiseptic, used as such by the French during the First World War.

## Dill

A hardy annual with thin, fine dark green leaves and yellow flowers. Dill grows happily in the garden in a sunny position. Sow from March to July, and pick leaves 8 weeks later. In the autumn you can either pick the seeds or let them self-seed.

The leaves, with an aniseed flavour, are used in fish dishes, in the bouillon for fish or shellfish, in fish and veal sauces, in spiced vinegar and butters, egg dishes and salads. Use as a garnish.

The stems and seeds are used to flavour pickling vinegar. Dill is very popular in Scandinavian cooking, traditionally used with raw, smoked and pickled salmon etc.

Freeze the green fronds for winter use, and store the seeds for a culinary or botanical use in air-tight jars.

When picking parsley for the autumn, rinse the clusters, pack in small plastic bags, and freeze. Alternatively, you can chop it up and freeze it in icecube trays, then place the green cubes in a plastic bag. Thawed parsley can be used as you would fresh. Parsley can also be grown indoors for winter use.

Parsley can be used in nearly anything, added at the last moment, finely chopped to flavour, as a major constituent of the classic bouquet garni, or as a garnish, fresh or deep fried.

## Thyme

A tiny, perennial plant with dark green leaves and lilac flowers, thyme thrives in sandy soil and needs a lot of sun. You can grow it in your window box for supplies throughout the winter. Pick when needed, and as leaves are evergreen, there is little to be gained by drying or freezing.

Use thyme in soups, in bouquets garnis, for meat, game and poultry, in marinades for salads and meat, in vegetable dishes, in spiced butter, and in pizzas and spaghetti dishes. You can also make herb tea with lemon thyme, related to common thyme.

## Rosemary

A beautiful, hardy, evergreen plant, rosemary leaves resemble pine needles and are sweetly fragrant. It thrives in a sunny sheltered position. Sow under glass or indoors in March. Pick leaves as needed, and dry for winter use.

Rosemary is most commonly used in bouquets garnis, with meat and fish dishes, with sauces and soups. Dried rosemary has a milder taste than fresh, but still use it sparingly.

## Tarragon

A hardy perennial herb, tarragon is a tall bushlike plant growing best in a sheltered position. French tarragon is better flavoured than Russian. One plant is enough for culinary use, so buy from a nursery and plant in October or March. Pick fresh leaves from mid June to end of September.

The thin, dark green leaves, fresh shoots and thin stems are used with fish dishes, with chicken and veal, with egg dishes, spiced butter and spiced vinegars, and with fresh chervil in a béarnaise sauce. Sprigs can be frozen or dried.

## Parsley

The most common of the herbs, parsley is a biennial, but is best grown as an annual as fewer and smaller leaves will be produced during the second year. Sow in March for summer and autumn use, and in July for winter and spring use.

## Basil

An annual herb, related to balm, with light green leaves and small white flowers. Basil thrives in a warm sheltered site, and in flowerpots indoors. Sow in March indoors, and pick leaves as required.

The clove-like flavour of the leaves

goes particularly well with tomato dishes, with pizzas and spaghetti, and is good with light meat and poultry, in salads, with liver pâté and pastes, with sausagemeat and spiced vinegar.

Basil can be frozen, although it loses some of its flavour, and can be dried, though not nearly so successfully. It's best to keep a plant on your windowsill throughout the winter.

## Sage

Sage is one of the few herbs to have been in constant use – in British cookery certainly – since the Middle Ages. A hardy evergreen, it grows best in a warm, dry position, as a decorative border, or in the herb garden. The leaves are wrinkled grey-green, and can be frozen or dried – but as leaves can be picked all year round, it is hardly worth the trouble.

Sage has a very strong spicy taste, and is used mainly as an ingredient in stuffings for fatty meat and poultry, and sometimes in pork sausages. Add to marinades, meat and vegetable soups and casseroles, to fish stock, and with liver and eels.

## Mint

The many varieties of mint give a huge range of flavours and scents – apple, ginger, peppermint etc – but the most common are green spearmint and round-leaved applemint. They grow almost anywhere, and will spread readily.

This is the traditional British herb, associated with fresh summer vegetables, lamb and mutton, mint sauce, with iced tea and other long cold drinks, and with salads.

Mint can be frozen or dried.

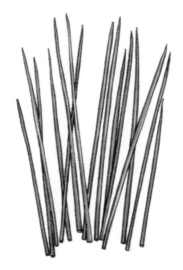

## Chives

A hardy perennial plant which will also grow anywhere and in anything. They need little attention, and are very easy to grow. Sow in March, and subdivide clumps every few years to make more plants.

Use chives with just about everything when you want to add their mild, fresh onion taste: with egg dishes, salads, casseroles, vegetables, potatoes and sandwiches. Chives can be frozen, but are best fresh.

## Bay Leaves

The sweet bay or bay laurel survives as a hardy shrub in all but the harshest of winters. Its green leaves have a sweet aromatic smell and flavour, and fresh leaves are stronger than dried. The dried leaves can be bought, but it is best to buy a small tree in a tub, and keep outside the kitchen door.

Bay leaves are invaluable in cooking, to flavour marinades, pickles, stocks and sauces, casseroles, pâtés and terrines. Its foremost use is in the classic bouquet garni.

# Step-by-Step
# Basic Casserole Rules

*The basic rules of all casseroles are largely the same. To illustrate this, we have chosen a goulash, pictured on the right, and in the small pictures below.*

**Goulash**
(serves 4)
Preparation time: 15–20 min.
Cooking time: 1½–2 hr
Suitable for the freezer

*About 400g (14oz) stewing (chuck) steak*
*4 onions*
*2 × 15ml tbsp (2tbsp) oil or 25g (1oz) butter or margarine*
*2 carrots*
*1 clove or garlic*
*1 green pepper*
*salt and black pepper*
*2–3 × 5ml tsp (2–3tsp) paprika*
*a pinch of cayenne pepper*
*1 large can of peeled tomatoes*
*250ml (9fl oz) light stock*
*1 small can tomato purée*
*1 × 15ml tbsp (1tbsp) cornflour*
*200ml (7fl oz) double or sour cream*

1 Cube meat. If you wish you could use half beef and half pork (shoulder or hand and spring). Peel onions and cut in thin slices. Scrape carrots and slice, clean pepper and slice.
2 Heat oil or butter in pan and brown first the onion rings and then the meat. Add carrots, crushed garlic, pepper and seasonings and spices. Stir well and turn heat down to low. Add stock, the canned tomatoes and their juice, and tomato purée.
3 Cover and leave to simmer until meat is tender. Thicken the meat juices with cornflour stirred in a little water, add double or sour cream and season to taste again if necessary. Serve goulash with boiled rice, creamy mashed potato or bread, and a bowl of salad.
This casserole freezes very well.

**STEP-BY-STEP**
*1 Cut meat into cubes. If you use two different types of meat, make sure they require the same cooking time.*

*2 Brown onions first, then meat. Add the spices before the liquid, but be careful not to let them burn.*

*3 When you have put meat, vegetables and spices in the pan, add liquid and leave casserole to simmer, covered, over low heat. Add vegetables needing only a short time to cook (cauliflower, broccoli, peas, green beans etc) shortly before meat is ready.*

*4 Add double or sour cream to gravy. Do this shortly before serving and after the thickening has been added. If you add cream too early, and let it boil, the gravy may curdle.*

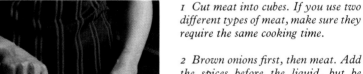

1

2

3

4

# Economical Beef Casseroles

*Shoulder cuts such as blade bone, clod or neck and chuck, and leg cuts such as brisket, shin, flank and leg, are good for braising and stewing in casseroles, and are fairly economical to buy.*

**Mexican Casserole** (above)
(serves 6–8)
Preparation time: about 20 min
Cooking time: 1½–2 hr
Suitable for the freezer

*about 1¼kg (about 3¼lb) stewing*
*steak*
*3–4 onions*
*2 cloves of garlic*
*4 × 15ml tbsp (4tbsp) oil*
*salt and pepper*
*500ml (just under 1pt) stock*
*1 paprika*

*6–8 ripe tomatoes or ½ large can*
*tomatoes*
*1 can white beans in tomato sauce*
*1–2 × 5ml tsp (1–2tsp) cornflour or*
*plain flour*
*½–1 × 5ml tsp (½–1tsp) chilli powder*
*or ¼ × 5ml tsp (¼tsp) cayenne*
*pepper*
*chopped parsley*

1 Cut meat into large cubes and remove gristle and most of the fat.
2 Sauté meat, chopped onions and crushed garlic in oil in a pan and sprinkle with salt, pepper and paprika. Add stock (perhaps from beef bones) and peeled quartered tomatoes. Cover and leave to simmer on low heat until meat is tender.
3 Add white beans in tomato sauce, bring back to boil and thicken with the flour mixed with 1–2 × 15ml tbsp (1–2tbsp) cold water.
4 Add chili powder or cayenne pepper when casserole is ready, but go easy with them – it's very easy to add too much.
Sprinkle with chopped parsley and serve with brown bread or rice.

**Skipper Stew**
Preparation time: about 15 min
Cooking time: about 2 hr
Suitable for the freezer

*About 1½kg (about 3¼lb) stewing*
*steak*
*1 litre (1¾pt) beef stock from bones*
*2 × 15ml tsp (2tsp) oil*
*2kg (4¼lb) potatoes*
*3–4 onions*
*salt, black peppercorns*
*50g (2oz) butter*
*1 sprig of parsley, 4 bay leaves*

1 When buying your meat, ask the butcher to give you some beef bones for making stock. Boil up with about 1 litre (1¾pt) water and 1 × 5ml tsp (1tsp) salt. Add other seasonings if you like – onions, peppercorns, celery, bay leaves etc. Skim off any scum, and strain after 1 hr.
2 Cut excess fat off meat, and cube. Sauté in pan in oil and ½ the butter. Add peeled, chopped potatoes, quartered onions, salt, 10–12 black peppercorns and bay leaves. Add the stock. Simmer until meat is tender

and potatoes nearly ready. Add more water or stock if necessary.

3 Stir in remaining butter when the stew is ready, and season to taste with more salt and pepper. Garnish with parsley and a knob of butter.

## Farmhouse Stew

(serves 6–8)
Preparation time: 25–30 min
Cooking time: about 2 hr
Suitable for the freezer

*1½kg (about 3¼lb) stewing steak*
*1½ litre (about 2½pt) beef stock (see previous recipe)*
*plain flour, salt, pepper*
*40g (1½oz) butter or 3 × 15ml tbsp (3tbsp) oil*
*5 carrots*
*½ celeriac or 2 stalks of celery*
*300ml (½pt) red wine or beef bone stock*
*4 leeks, 2 onions*
*1 sprig of parsley, 1 sprig of thyme, 2 bay leaves*

1 Make stock with bones and 1½ litre (about 2½pt) water, 2 × ml tsp (2tsp) salt, and other flavourings if you want (see previous recipe).

2 Cut excess fat off meat and cube. Place cubes in a plastic bag with 4–5 × 15ml tbsp (4–5tbsp) plain flour, 1 × 5ml tsp (1tsp) salt and ½ × 5ml tsp (½tsp) freshly ground black pepper. Shake well. Take meat cubes out of bag.

3 Sauté meat in butter and oil in a large pan. Turn down to low heat and add chopped onions, carrot slices, cubed celery and a bouquet garni consisting of green leek tops, parsley, thyme and bay leaves. Add about 1 litre (1¾pt) sieved stock. Cover, and leave to simmer until meat is tender. Add the white of the leeks, in chunks, and leave to cook with meat for the last 10–15 min.

## Potato Goulash (right)

(serves 6–8)
Preparation time: 15–20 min
Cooking time: 1–1½ hr
Suitable for the freezer

*100–200g (4–7oz) bacon or ham*
*1–1½kg (2¼–2¾lb) stewing steak*
*salt, pepper*
*marjoram, basil*
*1 can peeled tomatoes*
*4 onions, 8–10 potatoes*
*1 × 15ml tbsp (1tbsp) plain flour*

*about 550ml (1pt) stock (meat or vegetable)*
*15g (½oz) butter or margarine*
*2–3 × 5ml tsp (2–3tsp) paprika*
*100ml (4fl oz) double cream, chopped parsley*

1 Cut bacon or ham into thin slices and meat into large cubes. Heat an iron pot or saucepan and sauté meat and ham dry, stirring constantly so that they don't burn.

2 Turn down heat and add salt and pepper, dried or fresh herbs to taste, chopped onions and tomatoes. Add stock to cover meat, and leave to simmer, covered until nearly tender.

3 Cut peeled potatoes into cubes, place in pot and add more stock. Keep at a good simmer until potatoes are nearly done.

4 Mix butter with plain flour and paprika, and thicken gravy with this,

a little at a time, until you get the right consistency. Stir in cream, season to taste with salt, and garnish with chopped parsley.

## Chilli Pepper

The chilli pepper is a small, thin and very hot member of the sweet pepper or capsicum family. You can buy them fresh, but they are most commonly available dried or powdered – as chilli seasoning, chilli powder (which use the whole dried pod) or as cayenne pepper (which is the ground seeds).

Always add chilli – in whatever form – with caution. It is the seeds which are hottest, so if using fresh, the seeds can be removed before chopping flesh finely and adding to a casserole. Add powder or cayenne pepper only towards the end of cooking, and taste after 5 min.

# More Beefy Goodness

**Hungarian Goulash** (left)
(serves 4–6)
Preparation time: 15–20 min
Cooking time: 30–60 min, depending on quality of meat
Suitable for the freezer

*about 1kg (2¼lb) stewing steak*
*700–900g (1½–2lb) onions*
*1 clove of garlic*
*caraway seeds*
*50g (2oz) butter*
*550–700ml (1–1¼pt) beef stock*
*salt, black pepper, paprika*
*1 × 15ml tbsp (1tbsp) plain flour*

1 Remote any fat and gristle, and cut meat in fairly large chunks. Chop onions.
2 Sauté meat and onions a little at a time in most of the butter in frying pan and place in large pot or pan. Season.
Deglaze frying pan with most of the stock and pour into pot. Add crushed garlic and ½–1 × 5ml tsp (½–1tsp) crushed caraway seeds, cover and leave to simmer until meat is tender (very good steak will cook quicker). Add more stock if necessary.
3 Thicken with the flour and butter mixed, stirring in a little at a time until you get the right consistency. Season to taste.

**Beef in Red Wine**
(serves 4–6)
Preparation time: about 20 min
Cooking time: 30–60 min
Suitable for the freezer

*about 1kg (2¼lb) stewing steak*
*10–12 shallots or button onions*
*25g (1oz) butter or margarine*
*½ stalk of celery, 4–6 tomatoes*
*salt, pepper, basil, cress*
*500–600ml (about 1pt) red wine*
*250g (9oz) button mushrooms*

1 Cut meat into slices and rub with ground pepper.
2 Cut meat slices into strips and sauté with small whole onions in ½ the butter or margarine in large pan.
3 Turn heat down, and add sliced celery and tomato quarters. Sprinkle with salt, pepper and fresh or dried basil. Add red wine, cover and leave to simmer until meat is tender.

4 Sauté whole, cleaned mushrooms in remaining butter or margarine, season to taste with salt, and put into pot. Heat for a few moments before garnishing with chopped cress.

**Boeuf Stroganov** (above)
(serves 4)
Preparation time: about 20 min
Cooking time: 20 min
Not suitable for the freezer

*about 450g (1lb) very tender beef*
*(fillet or rump)*
*2 lemons, 2 large onions*
*40g (1½oz) butter or margarine*
*salt, pepper*
*250g (9oz) button mushrooms*

*150ml (¼pt) white wine*
*about 200ml (7fl oz) sour cream*

1 Slice meat and rub with ground black pepper and juice of 1 lemon. Slice onions. Clean mushrooms, slice and sprinkle with lemon juice.
2 Cut meat into strips, sauté quickly in 25g (1oz) butter in frying pan. Place in large pan and add salt.
3 Sauté onion rings and mushrooms in remaining butter, and mix with meat. Deglaze frying pan with wine and juice from remaining lemon and add finely grated lemon rind. Pour into saucepan with meat. Boil for a few minutes, then add sour cream and sprinkle with ground pepper.

10–15 min, adding more stock if necessary, and season to taste with more salt and pepper. Stir sour or double cream into gravy.

**Variation**
Replace the winter vegetables – parsnips, carrots, celeriac with, for instance, cauliflower, broccoli, green beans or corn.
You can also thicken the gravy with $\frac{1}{2}$–1 × 5ml tsp ($\frac{1}{2}$–1tsp) cornflour mixed with 100ml (4fl oz) cold stock.
Mashed potatoes garnished with finely chopped parsley, chives or cress is a nice substitute for bread.

**Winter Hotpot** (right)
(serves 6–8)
Preparation time: 15–20 min
Cooking time: about 2 hr
Suitable for the freezer.

*about 2kg (4¼lb) shin of beef, or*
  *brisket (on the bone)*
*25g (1oz) butter or margarine*
*4 onions, 6 carrots*
*½ celeriac or 2 stalks of celery*
*4–5 leeks*
*1 sprig of parsley*
*6–8 potatoes*
*salt and whole pepper*

1 Get your butcher to bone the meat, and cut it into 2.5cm (1in) thick slices.
2 Chop the onions and place at the bottom of a large fireproof casserole. Rub meat with salt and black pepper and place, with bones, on top of onion.
3 Make a bouquet garni of the green leek leaves, ½ sprig of parsley and a couple of leaves from the celeriac or celery. Place the bouquet garni in the pot and add boiling stock or water until meat is covered. Cover, and leave pot to simmer until meat is tender. Skim if necessary.
4 Remove bouquet garni, and remove bones. Take out any marrow and whisk well into meat juices.
5 Place scraped, sliced vegetables in pot and add more stock or water, salt and pepper, and leave to cook until vegetables are ready.
6 Remove meat and cut into small cubes, removing any bones, gristle or excess fat. Put meat back into pot and cook until everything is piping hot. Sprinkle with parsley.
Serve straight from the casserole dish with brown rye bread.

# For Cold Days

*These dishes take a long time to cook, but need no looking after.*

**Esterhazy Goulash** (above)
(serves 6–8)
Preparation time: 15–20 min
Cooking time: 1½–2 hr
Suitable for the freezer

*1½–2kg (3¾–4¼lb) stewing steak (or*
  *brisket)*
*6 onions*
*4 × 15ml tbsp (4tbsp) oil or 50g*
  *(2oz) butter*
*salt, black, pepper, paprika*
*thyme, rosemary, 4–5 juniper berries*
*2 bay leaves*
*1 litre (1¾pt) stock*

*6 carrots, 1 parsnip*
*½ celeriac or 2 stalks of celery*
*3–4 × 15ml tbsp (3–4tbsp) sour or*
  *double cream*

1 Cut meat in fairly large cubes and remove any bones and gristle. Leave fat during the cooking, and cut away when casserole is ready if you wish.
2 Brown meat and onion rings in oil or butter. Add 1 × 5ml tsp (1tsp) salt, ¼ × 5ml tsp (¼tsp) pepper, ½–1 × 15ml tbsp (½–1tbsp) paprika, 2–3 × 5ml tsp (2–3tsp) fresh or 1 × 5ml tsp (1tsp) dried thyme and rosemary, crushed juniper berries and bay leaves.
3 Pour enough stock into pot to nearly cover the meat, cover, and simmer until meat is nearly tender.
4 Wash, scrape or peel vegetables and slice into thick julienne strips. Put in the casserole for the last

# Cast-iron Cooking

*One of the best pans to use for braising or stewing is a cast-iron casserole with a tight-fitting lid. It can be used to fry and braise, it holds heat well and you can bring it to the table for serving.*

**Pepper Casserole** (left)
(serves 6–8)
Preparation time: about 15 min
Cooking time: about 1½ hr
Suitable for the freezer

1–1½kg (2¼–3¼lb) stewing steak
450g (1lb) onions
50g (2oz) butter or margarine
salt, pepper
1–2 × 15ml tbsp (1–2tbsp) paprika
1 lemon
1 can tomato purée
1 litre (1¾pt) stock
1 × 5ml tsp (1tsp) dried thyme
700–900g (1½–2lb) small potatoes
2–3 green and 1 red pepper
8 ripe tomatoes or ½ large can
    tomatoes
1–2 × 5ml tsp (1–2tsp) cornflour

1 Brown chopped onion in butter or margarine in the pot together with large cubes of beef. Turn down the heat and add salt, pepper, paprika, lemon juice, tomato purée, stock and thyme. Cover, and leave to simmer on low heat for about 1 hr.
2 Place small, peeled potatoes in pot and leave to cook for 15–20 min. Add chopped peppers and peeled tomatoes and continue to cook until everything is tender.
3 Season to taste again, and add grated lemon rind. Thicken gravy with cornflour mixed with a little cold water.
Serve hot with brown bread and a nice, simple green salad.

**Oxtail Ragôut** (left)
(serves 6–8)
Preparation time: 20–25 min
Cooking time: about 2½ hr
Suitable for the freezer

2–2½kg (4¼–5½lb) oxtail
50g (2oz) butter or margarine
2 onions
salt, pepper, paprika
3 × 15ml tbsp (3tbsp) tomato purée

$2 \times 15ml$ tbsp ( 2tbsp ) plain flour
$\frac{1}{2}$ bottle red wine
300–400ml ($\frac{1}{2}$–$\frac{3}{4}$pt) stock
1 bay leaf
$1 \times 5ml$ tsp ( 1tsp ) dried thyme
4–5 carrots
$\frac{1}{4}$ celeriac or 1 stalk of celery
3 leeks
250g ( 9oz ) small mushrooms
about 200ml ( 7fl oz ) sour or double
  cream
parsley

1 Wash the oxtail joints, dip in boiling water for a short time, and remove excess fat.
2 Brown meat and chopped onions in about $\frac{1}{2}$ the butter or margarine, turn heat down, and sprinkle with salt, pepper and paprika.
3 Mix tomato purée and flour, add red wine and stock and pour mixture into pot. Add crushed bay leaf and thyme, bring to the boil, and leave to simmer for about 2 hrs, covered.
4 Chop up scraped carrots, celeriac or celery and leeks finely, place in pot, and leave to cook for about

20 min. Slice cleaned mushrooms in half, sauté in frying pan in remaining butter or margarine, and season to taste. Place in pot.
5 Mix sour or double cream with salt, pepper and plenty of finely chopped parsley. Garnish the ragôut with this just before serving, or stir into it. Serve hot with boiled or mashed potatoes, or white bread.

**Settlers' Casserole** (above)
(serves 6–8)
Preparation time: 15–20 min
Cooking time: about 1$\frac{1}{2}$ hr
Suitable for the freezer

1$\frac{1}{2}$–2kg ( 3$\frac{1}{4}$–4$\frac{1}{2}$lb ) rump steak
$4 \times 15ml$ tbsp ( 4tbsp ) oil or 50g
  ( 2oz ) butter
3 onions
1 clove of garlic, salt, pepper
paprika, caraway seeds
$\frac{1}{2}$ sprig of parsley
fresh or dried basil
4 carrots
$\frac{1}{4}$ celeriac or 1 stalk of celery
4 leeks

8 tomatoes or $\frac{1}{2}$ medium can of
  tomatoes
700–900ml ( 1$\frac{1}{4}$–1$\frac{1}{2}$pt ) stock

1 Cut meat into fairly large cubes and rub with ground black pepper.
2 Brown meat, chopped onions and crushed garlic in the oil or butter in a large pot. Sprinkle with salt, paprika and crushed caraway seeds, and add stock. Make bouquet garni of parsley, basil, celery or celeriac leaves and green of the leeks, and place in pot. (If you fasten it to the pot handle with twine or string, it will be a lot easier to remove.) Leave to simmer until meat is nearly tender.
3 Wash, scrape or peel all vegetables (except the tomatoes) and slice finely. Remove bouquet garni, place vegetables in pot and cook until ready.
4 Scald, peel and halve tomatoes and put in the casserole for the last 6–8 min. Season to taste again if necessary.
Serve with boiled potatoes garnished with parsley, or brown bread.

*Above : Cod with Mushrooms and Cream.*     *Below : Fish and Shellfish Casserole.*

# Cod Casseroles

*Cod is a tasty fish to casserole, and makes a change from frying or baking.*

### Cod with Mushrooms and Cream
(serves 4–6)
Preparation time: about 15 min
Cooking time: 15–20 min
Suitable for the freezer

$\frac{3}{4}$–1kg ($1\frac{3}{4}$–$2\frac{1}{4}$lb) cod fillets
salt, pepper
25g (1oz) butter or margarine
1 lemon
2 onions, fresh or dried tarragon
300ml ($\frac{1}{2}$pt) white wine or fish stock
250g (9oz) mushrooms
200ml (7fl oz) single cream, parsley

1 Sprinkle cod fillets with salt and juice of $\frac{1}{2}$ lemon. Place in a cool place. Clean mushrooms, slice and

sprinkle with lemon juice.

2 Melt butter or margarine in a flameproof dish or casserole, place chopped onion on the bottom with the cod fillets on top. Sprinkle with I × 15ml tbsp (1tbsp) or I × 5ml tsp (1tsp) dried tarragon and finely grated lemon rind. Add wine or fish stock, cover with lid or doubled tin-foil and steam until tender on a low heat.

3 Add mushrooms and cream just before the fish is ready. Leave the dish to simmer for about 4–5 min, uncovered, and season to taste with salt and pepper. Sprinkle with chopped parsley.

Serve hot with French bread or boiled potatoes.

VARIATION:

Cut cod fillets into small chunks, turn in seasoned flour, and brown until golden in butter or margarine. Brown onion and mushrooms and place all ingredients in layers in a pot. Add wine or fish stock, lemon juice and grated lemon rind as well as herbs and spices and leave to simmer for about 10 min. Add warmed cream just before serving.

## Fried Cod Casserole

(serves 4–6)
Preparation time: about 15 min
Cooking time: 15–20 min
Suitable for the freezer

*6 cod fillets, salt, pepper*
*I egg, plain flour, breadcrumbs*
*butter or margarine*
*100g (4oz) bacon, 2–3 onions*
*I can peeled tomatoes, I lemon*
*100g (4oz) fresh or frozen peas*
*parsley*

1 Dry cod fillets and turn in flour, mixed with salt and pepper, then in whisked egg and finally bread-crumbs.

2 Fry cod fillets in butter or mar-garine and place in serving dish. Brown bacon cubes and chopped onions and put in pot.

3 Deglaze the frying pan with the tomatoes and their juice, and pour this into the pot with the peas. Season with a little salt and pepper, and leave to summer for about 10 min under lid. Sprinkle with grated lemon rind and finely chopped parsley to garnish.

Serve with boiled potatoes or rice.

## Fish and Shellfish Casserole

(serves 4–6)
Preparation time: 25–30 min
Cooking time: about 40 min in all
Not suitable for the freezer

*1kg (2¼lb) fresh mussels*
*450–700g (1–1½lb) cod fillets*
*about 200g (7oz) fresh scallops*
*450–700g (1–1½lb) boiled lobster or*
*    same weight of crab meat*
*salt, 8 black peppercorns*
*I bay leaf, 2 cloves of garlic*
*½ sprig of parsley*
*300ml (½pt) white wine*
*200–300ml (7–10fl oz) fish stock*
*4 onions*
*2–3 × 15ml tbsp (2–3tbsp) olive oil*
*saffron or turmeric*

1 Rinse and prepare mussels and place in boiling white wine and fish stock. Add I × 5ml tsp (1tsp) salt, pepper, bay leaf, parsley and I clove of garlic. Cover and boil, shaking the pan frequently. Any shells which do not open after 5–6 min should be discarded. Set some of the mussels aside in their shells, and remove meat from the rest. Sieve the stock.

2 Brown chopped onions and re-maining crushed garlic until nice and golden in oil. Add cod fillets cut into small pieces, a pinch of saffron or ½ × 5ml tsp (½tsp) turmeric, scal-lops and the sieved stock from the mussels. Leave everything to simmer on low heat until fish is tender.

3 Place mussels with and without shells and lobster or crab meat in the pot, leave until warmed through, and season to taste with salt and pepper.

## Cod Bake

(serves 4)
Preparation time: 10 min
Cooking time: about 15 min
Suitable for the freezer

*4 cod fillets*
*salt, pepper*
*8 boiled potatoes*
*50g (2oz) butter*
*I lemon, I onion, 2 leeks*
*1–2 × 5ml tsp (1–2tsp) mustard*
*I sprig of parsley*
*100ml (4fl oz) fish or light stock*

1 Rub cod fillets with salt and pepper, slice into small pieces and place in layers in a pot with thick slices of cooked, cold potatoes and thin, raw leek rings.

2 Mix melted butter with lemon juice, finely chopped onion, mus-tard, fish stock, finely chopped pars-ley and a little salt and pepper. Pour mixture into pot, cover, and simmer until fish is done.

# More Fishy Feasts

*With judicious buying from a fishmonger, you can make delicious, tempting casseroles.*

## Summer Fish Casserole

(serves 4–6)
Preparation time: about 20 min
Cooking time: about 30 min in all
Suitable for the freezer

*700–900g (1½–2lb) fish fillets*
*1 lemon*
*2 onions, 2 leeks*
*2 × 15ml tbsp (2tbsp) oil*
*1 head of fennel, 1 cauliflower*
*2 carrots, 1 pepper*
*¼ litre (9fl oz) fish stock*
*¼ litre (9fl oz) white wine*
*saffron or turmeric*
*salt, cayenne pepper*
*200–400g (7–14oz) shrimps*
*parsley, sage*

1 Prepare and cut vegetables into small sections, all about the same size. Choose a firm fish like cod, turbot or halibut. Sprinkle with salt and lemon juice.
2 Brown onion and leek in oil until golden. Add the remaining vegetables, fish stock, wine, a pinch of saffron or 1 × 5ml tsp (1tsp) turmeric and a small pinch of cayenne pepper. Cover, and simmer for 10–15 min.
3 Cut fish into small bits, place in casserole and steam until tender. Add shrimps, salt, a little more cayenne pepper (but go carefully), chopped parsley and a pinch of fresh or dried sage.

VARIATION
Fennel goes well with fish, but you could use celery instead.

## Plaice Casserole

(serves 4–6)
Preparation time: about 15 min
Cooking time: about 1 hr in all
Suitable for the freezer

*700–900g (1½–2lb) plaice*
*1 lemon, 2 onions*
*salt, black peppercorns*
*4 leeks, 2 sprigs of parsley*
*1 bay leaf, 300ml (½pt) white wine*
*40g (1½oz) butter or margarine*
*1 × 15ml tbsp (1tbsp) plain flour*
*250ml (9fl oz) cream*
*100g (4oz) cream cheese*
*chives, lemon balm*

1 Ask your fishmonger to fillet the fish for you, but keep the bones etc, as you need them to make stock.
Boil in 200–300ml (7–10fl oz) water with chopped onion, sliced lemon, salt, 8 black peppercorns, green top of leek, ½ sprig of parsley and bay leaf. Simmer for 30 min and sieve.
2 Chop leeks and use as much of the green part as possible. Steam in 25g (1oz) butter on low heat for 10 min. Rub fish fillets with salt, roll them up from the tail end, and fasten with wooden cocktail sticks. Place fish rolls in a pot, pour stock and white wine over fish, cover, and poach for about 10 min.

*Left: Delicious Summer Fish Casserole.*

3 Mix remaining soft butter with flour and cheese, stir into stock gradually and simmer on low heat, stirring continuously, until stock is smooth. Add cream, and season to taste with herbs and spices.

VARIATION
The dish can be made a bit simpler by using frozen fish fillets and mushrooms – or canned asparagus soup, diluted with a little white wine. This does not require the flour and cheese thickening.

**Fish with Tomatoes and Mushrooms** (below)
(serves 4–6)
Preparation time: about 15 min
Cooking time: about 30 min in all
Suitable for the freezer

*700–900g (1½–2lb) fish fillets*
*1 lemon*
*50–100g (2–4oz) bacon*
*25g (1oz) butter or margarine*
*3 large onions, 1–2 cloves of garlic*
*1 × 15ml tbsp (1tbsp) plain flour*
*1 green pepper*
*6 ripe tomatoes or ½ can of tomatoes*
*1 small can tomato purée*
*225–450g (½–1lb) mushrooms*
*caraway seeds*
*salt, pepper, paprika*

1 Sprinkle lemon juice and salt on fish fillets.
2 Fry bacon cubes until golden in ½ the butter or margarine. Remove from pan, then sauté chopped onions and crushed garlic. Stir in flour, leave to sauté for a minute or two, then add tomato purée, sliced pepper and quartered peeled tomatoes and their juice. If you are using fresh tomatoes, add 200ml (7fl oz) stock, tomato juice or water.

Cover, and simmer for 15 min.
3 Slice fish fillets into strips and place in the pot with the tomato sauce. Sauté halved, cleaned mushrooms in remaining butter and season to taste with salt and lemon juice. Place into pot along with the bacon cubes and add salt, pepper, paprika and whole or crushed caraway seeds. Leave to simmer on low heat until fish is tender.
Serve with potatoes garnished with parsley.

VARIATION
Use frozen, mixed vegetables with peas, beans, corn and pepper instead of mushrooms, and serve dish in a ring of boiled rice.

**Plaice in Shrimp Sauce**
(serves 4–6)
Preparation time: about 30 min
Cooking time: about 20 min
Suitable for the freezer

*8–12 plaice fillets, salt and pepper*
*225–450g (½–1lb) shrimps*
*1 sprig of parsley*
*fresh or dried dill*
*75g (3oz) butter*
*200ml (7fl oz) fish stock*
*1 lemon*
*100–200ml (4–7fl oz) white wine*
*100–200ml (4–7oz) cream*
*2 × 15ml tbsp (2tbsp) plain flour*
*2 egg yolks*

1 Rub plaice fillets with salt and leave in a cool place for about 10 min.
2 Peel shrimps and crush shells in a mortar or bowl. Sauté shrimp shells for 10 min in butter on low heat and sieve butter through a fine-mesh sieve. Discard shells.
3 Place some of the shrimps on the fish fillets and roll up. Fasten with wooden cocktail sticks. Poach fillets in fish stock with lemon juice, white wine and dill until compact and white.
4 Make a sauce of shrimp butter, plain flour and sieved fish stock. Simmer, stirring, for a few minutes then whisk in the cream and egg yolks which have been mixed together with some of the hot sauce. Add the remaining shrimps, dill, salt and pepper. Pour sauce over fish rolls and heat carefully on a low heat. Garnish with parsley.
Serve hot with French bread or boiled potatoes.

# Halibut and Sole Casseroles

*Expensive, but delicious, halibut and sole are in a class of their own.*

### Halibut in Wine Sauce
(below)
(serves 4–6)
Preparation time: 15–20 min
Cooking time: about 30 min in all
Suitable for the freezer, but loses some flavour.

*about 1 kg (2¼ lb) halibut fillets*
*½ lemon, 4 shallots or small onions*
*1 clove of garlic, 1 carrot*
*2 thin leeks, 6 small tomatoes*
*100g (4oz) butter or margarine*
*250g (9oz) button mushrooms*
*salt, white pepper, paprika*
*saffron or turmeric*
*300 ml (½pt) dry white wine*

1 Rub fish fillets with salt and sprinkle with lemon juice.
2 Sauté chopped shallots or onions, crushed garlic, grated carrot and finely sliced leeks for about 10 min in butter or margarine on low heat. Scald and peel tomatoes, cut in four, and sauté for about 5 min in butter.
3 Place whole or sliced fillets in pot with whole, washed mushrooms and sprinkle with salt, pepper, paprika and a pinch of saffron or ½ × 5ml tsp (½tsp) turmeric. Add the dry white wine and cover. Poach fish on low heat for about 10–20 min, depending on thickness of fillets.
Serve with hot French bread.

### Saffron and Turmeric
In a lot of the recipes you will find that either saffron or turmeric can be used. They are quite different spices, but have roughly the same effect, as both have a delicate yellow colour and a nice, round taste. Saffron is the stigmas of crocuses found around the Mediterranean. It is best to buy saffron whole, when it resembles small, reddish brown threads. It is very expensive – not really surprising as it takes thousands of stigmas to make 25g (1oz) – but it lasts a long time.
Turmeric is the powdered root of a ginger-type plant. It does not taste like ginger – it has hardly any taste at all – but it adds a nice yellow colour to casseroles, rice dishes, sauces etc, and is nowhere near as expensive as saffron. It is turmeric which gives the mixed spices of curry powder the yellow colour.

### Gratin of Sole (right)
(serves 4)
Preparation time: about 20 min
Cooking time: 20–25 min
Not suitable for the freezer

*4 soles*
*salt, 1 lemon*
*4 shallots or small onions*
*50–75g (2–3oz) butter or margarine*
*200ml (7fl oz) dry white wine*

*white pepper*
*225–450g (½–1lb) fresh button*
*mushrooms*
*250ml (9fl oz) double or sour cream*
*2 egg yolks*
*2 × 15ml tbsp (2tbsp) grated cheese*

1 Skin and fillet soles (see below). Rub with salt and sprinkle with the juice from ½ lemon.
2 Sauté finely chopped onions for 8–10 min in butter or margarine on low heat, then add sole fillets, cleaned, sliced mushrooms, salt, pepper, white wine and the rest of the lemon juice. Cover and poach fish until tender for about 10 min.
3 Mix egg yolks with double or sour cream and grated cheese. Pour mixture over fish and place pan or dish under grill or in a hot oven (240°C, 475°F, Gas 9) for a few minutes until surface is light gold in colour. Serve hot with boiled potatoes or French bread.

VARIATION
You can make this dish with other kinds of fish – plaice for instance. Instead of mushrooms you can use chopped fennel which goes well with fish and cheese.

## Sole Florentine
(serves 4)
Preparation time: 20–25 min
Cooking time: 15–20 min
Suitable for the freezer, but quality will deteriorate

*6–8 sole fillets*
*salt, pepper*
*1 packet frozen spinach*

**How to Skin Flat Fish:**
*1 Using a very sharp knife, make an incision across the tail on the dark skin side of the fish. The white skin on the other side is usually left on.*

*grated nutmeg*
*4–6 shallots or small onions*
*40g (1½oz) butter*
*200ml (7fl oz) dry white wine*
*100g (4oz) cream cheese*
*100ml (4fl oz) double cream*
*1 lemon*

1 Rub fish fillets with salt and leave for about 10 min.
2 Thaw spinach in a colander and then steam for 6–8 min in 15g (½oz) butter, 1 × 15ml tbsp (1tbsp) water, salt, pepper and nutmeg.

*2 Slip the thumbs into the slit and gently loosen the skin, and work your way down the sides by the fins until it is free all round.*

3 Sauté finely chopped onions in butter in a low, wide flameproof pan or dish for about 5 min. Fold fillets and place in pan. Add white wine and steam fish for about 8–10 min under a lid or doubled tinfoil.
4 Place spinach in a ring around the edge of the dish. Mix the cream cheese with double cream, salt and pepper. Pour mixture over fish and heat for a couple of minutes with the lid on.
Garnish with lemon and serve with French bread.

*3 Hold the tail firmly, and pull the skin quickly towards the head. You may need the sharp knife to help you on your way.*

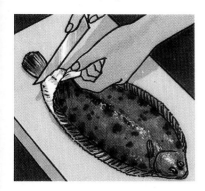

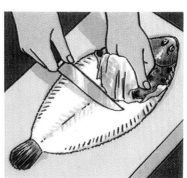

# Everyday Fish Casseroles

*Amongst the more tasty – and more economical – are mackerel, haddock and herring. They, too, can be made into delicious casseroles.*

## Fisherman's Casserole

(serves 4–6)
Preparation time: 10–15 min
Cooking time: 1 hr in all
Suitable for the freezer

*4–6 medium haddock*
*1 large onion, 1 carrot*
*1 bay leaf, ½ sprig parsley*
*2 × 5ml tsp (2tsp) vinegar, 4 black*
*    peppercorns, 4 mustard seeds*
*salt, pepper*
*10–12 shallots or button onions*
*2 green peppers*
*25g (1oz) butter or margarine*
*1 × 15ml tbsp (1tbsp) plain flour*
*3 × 15ml tbsp (3tbsp) tomato purée*
*¼ × 5ml tsp (¼tsp) dried thyme*
*4 ripe tomatoes*

1 Fillet the haddock and make a fish stock, using the head and bones, about ½ litre (about 1pt) water, vinegar, chopped onion, carrot, bay leaf, parsley, 1 × 5ml tsp (1tsp) salt, 4 black peppercorns and 4 mustard seeds. Simmer stock for about 30 min, covered, then sieve.
2 Rub fillets with salt and slice lengthways or in cubes.
3 Peel the small onions and slice and chop peppers. Brown both in butter, stir in plain flour and gradually add fish stock and tomato purée. Boil for about 10 min. Place fish slices and peeled quartered tomatoes into the pot and leave to simmer on low heat until fish is firm.
4 Season to taste with crushed thyme and salt and pepper if necessary.

VARIATION
Freshwater fish like perch and pike are ideally suited for this kind of casserole. They are more difficult to fillet, though, so cook fish whole in stock, before removing skin and bones. Place the cooked fish fillets in the prepared vegetable mixture and boil stock separately.

## Curried Herring Casserole

(serves 4)
Preparation time: 15–20 min
Cooking time: about 20 min in all
Suitable for the freezer

*½kg (1lb 2oz) fresh herring fillets*
*salt, pepper, curry powder*
*2 large onions, 1 large apple*
*25g (1oz) butter or margarine*
*1 × 15ml tbsp (1tbsp) plain flour*
*300–400ml (½–¾pt) fish stock*
*100–200ml (4–7fl oz) double cream*
*dill*
*225g (½lb) fresh or frozen peas*

1 Rinse fillets, dry and rub with salt. Roll together around a sprig of dill and fasten with wooden cocktail sticks.
2 Sauté finely chopped onions until smooth in butter on low heat. Add 1–2 × 5ml tsp (1–2tsp) curry powder and small peeled apple cubes. Stir in flour and simmer for a while, before adding fish stock. Leave to simmer for 8–10 min.
3 Mix cream into stock, season to taste with salt and pepper, and place herring rolls and peas in the pot. Cook on low heat until fish is firm and white all the way through. Garnish with dill.

VARIATION
Boil stock with onions, but without curry and apple. Add about 100g (4oz) finely chopped parsley, dill or chives and season to taste with lemon juice or vinegar. Garnish with 1 chopped, hard-boiled egg.

## TIPS
### Herring smell
After filleting herring, it can be difficult to remove the smell from the knife, working surface or board, and your fingers. Rub with a cloth dipped in vinegar, or add some vinegar to the washing-up water. This simple remedy will remove all smells, but do remember to rinse thoroughly in cold water afterwards.

## Mackerel Casserole

(serves 4)
Preparation time: about 20 min
Cooking time: about 30 min
Suitable for the freezer

*2–3 fresh mackerel*
*1 lemon, salt, pepper*
*1 bay leaf*

*2 × 15ml tbsp (2tbsp) oil*
*8 small potatoes, 1 clove of garlic*
*1 onion, 4 thin leeks, parsley*
*¼ litre (9fl oz) fish stock*
*200ml (7fl oz) double cream*
*1 sprig of dill*

1 Fillet the mackerel. Boil head and bones in water, with salt, pepper, onion, parsley and bay leaf to make stock. Rub fillets with a dash of salt and sprinkle with the juice of ½ lemon.
2 Peel potatoes and slice thinly. Cut the leek into rings.
3 Heat oil in a wide, lidded frying pan. Place potatoes, fish fillets and leek in layers in pot and sprinkle with salt, pepper, finely grated lemon rind and crushed garlic between layers. Pour rest of lemon juice and fish stock on top, cover, and simmer on low heat for about 30 min.
4 Add cream, mixed with chopped dill. The potatoes will have by now absorbed most of the liquid. Leave dish until thoroughly heated, and serve with brown bread.

## Oven-baked Fish Casserole

(serves 4)
Preparation time: about 5 min
Cooking time: 20–30 min
Oven temperature: 240°C, 475°F, Gas 9
Suitable for the freezer

*700g (1½lb) haddock of cod fillets*
*about 75g (3oz) butter or margarine,*
*    melted*
*2 × 15ml tbst (2tbsp) lemon juice*
*1 × 5ml tsp (1tsp) dry mustard*
*a pinch of pepper*
*1½ × 5ml tsp (1½tsp) salt*
*breadcrumbs, paprika*

1 Cover bottom of ovenproof dish with breadcrumbs and place fish fillets on top.
2 Mix butter, lemon juice, mustard, pepper and salt and pour mixture over fish. Sprinkle with a little paprika.
3 Cook dish for about 20–30 min in the hot oven. Baste with juices which will collect in the dish during cooking.
Serve with a green salad and mashed potato.

*Haddock, as used in Fisherman's Casserole, is ideal for this type of dish.*

# Lamb or Mutton Casseroles

*Mutton, if you can find it, has a special taste, which is delicious in casseroles, as also is lamb. All these recipes take a long time to cook, therefore the cheaper cuts can be used successfully.*

**Marinated Lamb Casserole**
(serves 6–8)
Preparation time: about 20 min
Marination time: about 12 hrs
Cooking time: about 1 hr
Suitable for the freezer

50–100g (2–4oz) salt ham
about 1½kg (3¾lb) stewing lamb or
  mutton (a neck cut)
4 carrots
¼ celeriac or 2 stalks of celery
4 leeks
250g (9oz) button mushrooms
For the marinade:
2 × 15ml tbsp (2tbsp) oil
2 onions, 2 cloves of garlic
300ml (½pt) white wine
1 sprig of parsley
1 bay leaf, 1 sprig of thyme
salt, black peppercorns

1 Cut the ham into small cubes and the lamb or mutton into larger cubes. Mix a marinade of oil, wine, chopped onions, crushed garlic and 8 black peppercorns. Pour it over the ham and meat cubes, and place a bouquet garni in the pot, consisting of the top of a leek, ½ sprig of parsley, bay leaf and thyme. Cover with lid or plastic film, and leave to chill for about 12 hr or overnight.
2 Scrape vegetables clean and chop. If you are using an earthenware pot, leave it in cold water for about 10–15 min (do not dry afterwards). Place meat and all vegetables in pot, except mushrooms, sprinkle with salt and pour marinade (without bouquet garni) over.
3 Cover pot with lid and place on a grid over low heat, or in the oven at 180°C, 350°F, Gas 4. Leave to simmer until meat is tender. Add mushrooms during the last 8–10 min.
4 Season to taste with salt and pepper and sprinkle with chopped parsley.
Serve with brown bread.

VARIATION
You can marinate the meat in tomato juice and cook with canned tomatoes. Replace bay leaf and thyme with basil and marjoram and serve with baked potatoes or boiled rice.

**Stuffed Cabbage**
(serves 6–8)
Preparation time: 25–30 min
Cooking time: about 1 hr
Suitable for the freezer

450–700g (1–1½lb) boneless lamb or
  mutton
150g (5oz) bacon rashers
1 cabbage
2 onions
2 × 15ml tbsp (2tbsp) cornflour
salt, pepper

2 eggs
100ml (4fl oz) cream, stock
paprika, marjoram, nutmeg
1 × 15ml tbsp (1tbsp) capers
finely chopped parsley
soy sauce, sour cream
dill

1 Cut about 12–16 large leaves carefully off cabbage and remove some of the stem to allow the leaves to lie flat. Boil leaves for about 5 minutes in lightly salted water.
2 Mince the lamb or mutton yourself or ask your butcher to do it for you. Season mince well with salt. Add grated onions, cornflour, ½ × 5ml tsp (½tsp) pepper, eggs, cream, 1 × 5ml tsp (1tsp) paprika, a pinch of crushed marjoram, a dash of nutmeg and the capers. Add stock a little at a time and stir well so that the mince absorbs all the liquid.
3 Divide the mince between the cabbage leaves, fold the sides over, and roll up. Place an unglazed earthenware dish in cold water for about 10–15 min. Place ½ the bacon rashers on the bottom of the dish with cabbage rolls on top. Cut the rest of the bacon in two and place in between rolls.

4 Add soy sauce to taste to 300–400 ml (½–¾pt) stock, pour into dish, and replace lid. Place pot on grid over low heat, or in the oven at 200°C, 400°F, Gas 6, for about 1 hr.
5 Pour off the meat juices. If they seem thin, add a little thickening. Stir in 100–200ml (4–7fl oz) sour cream and finely chopped dill. Pour gravy over rolls before serving.
Serve with boiled rice or boiled potatoes garnished with finely chopped parsley.

VARIATION
Mix 50–100g (2–4oz) cooked rice with mince and replace capers and parsley with 1 chopped red pepper. The stock can be replaced with tomato juice, mixed with a little white wine.

**Lamb Fricassée**
(serves 6–8)
Preparation time: 20–25 min
Cooking time: 1–1½ hr
Suitable for the freezer

1½–2kg (3¼–4½lb) lamb or mutton
  (shoulder or neck, on the bone)
1 onion, 1 parsnip
8 carrots, 1 leek

25g (1oz) butter
3 × 15ml tbsp (3tbsp) plain flour
450g (1lb) fresh or frozen peas
250ml (9fl oz) double cream
salt, pepper, parsley

1 Place meat whole in large pan or dish, and cover with water. Bring to the boil and skim off scum. Add 1 × 5ml tsp (1tsp) salt and leave meat to boil for another 45 min. Add onion, parsnip, carrots, leek and bouquet garni made from the green part of the leek and ½ sprig of parsley. Leave pot to simmer until meat is tender.
2 Sieve stock, remove bouquet garni and chop up the boiled vegetables. Cut meat into cubes and remove all bones and gristle.
3 Melt butter in a pan, add flour, and make a sauce with meat stock and cream. Stir continuously until smooth. Add peas and bring to the boil. Place the meat and the rest of the vegetables in the sauce and heat thoroughly. Season to taste with salt and pepper and add finely chopped parsley.

Opposite: Stuffed Cabbage.
Below: Marinated Lamb Casserole.

# Lamb and Vegetable Stews

*Lamb can be mixed with a variety of vegetables and herbs to make deliciously different stews.*

**Colourful Lamb Stew** (right)
(serves 6–8)
Preparation time: about 20 min
Cooking time: 1–1½ hr
Suitable for the freezer

*about 1½kg (about 3¼lb) lamb*
  *(boned shoulder or neck)*
*2 × 15ml tbsp (2tbsp) oil, salt,*
  *pepper*
*2 large onions*
*2 × 15ml tbsp (2tbsp) plain flour*
*½ litre (about 1pt) tomato juice*
*6 carrots*
*10–12 shallots or pickling onions*
*250g (9oz) fresh or frozen peas*
*250g (9oz) green beans, 6 tomatoes*
*parsley, basil*

1 Cut meat into small chunks, rub with pepper and fry in oil with chopped onions.
2 Sprinkle with 1 × 5ml tsp (1tsp) salt and the plain flour and gradually add tomato juice. Stir well, bring to the boil, and simmer on low heat for about 45 min, covered.
3 Add sliced carrots and whole peeled onions and simmer for a further 10–15 min.
4 Add peas, beans, peeled, quartered tomatoes, salt and pepper as well as finely chopped parsley and basil. Leave to cook until everything is tender adding more tomato juice if necessary (or use water if preferred).

**Irish Stew**
(serves 6–8)
Preparation time: 20–25 min
Cooking time: about 1½ hr
Suitable for the freezer

*about 1½kg (3¼lb) middle neck of*
  *lamb*
*coarse sea salt, black peppercorns*
*10–12 medium potatoes*
*2 large onions*
*4 leeks, 4–6 carrots*
*1 sprig of parsley*

1 Cut meat into fairly large cubes.

Peel and slice the vegetables.
2 Place meat and vegetables in layers in a pot or casserole dish with salt and peppercorns in between. Add about 1½ litre (about 2½ pt) boiling water or vegetable stock, cover, and leave to simmer on low heat until meat is tender.
3 Add more liquid if necessary during cooking time. Some of the potato slices can be mashed to thicken the meat juices. Sprinkle with a little parsley.
Serve hot with bread.

**Lamb Goulash**
(serves 6–8)
Preparation time: 20–25 min
Cooking time: 1½ hr
Suitable for the freezer

*about 1½kg (3¼lb) boned lamb*
  *shoulder*
*4 onions*
*1 clove of garlic*
*25–40g (1–1½oz) butter*
*salt, pepper, paprika, caraway seeds*

*4 carrots, 4–6 tomatoes*
*1 green and 1 red pepper*
*3–4 leeks*
*400ml (¾pt) stock (from bones)*
*200–300ml (7–10fl oz) red wine*
*sour or double cream*

1 Cut meat into chunks. Make a stock from the bones as described on page 16. Brown meat with chopped onions and crushed garlic in the butter. Sprinkle with seasonings and spices and add stock. Leave to simmer for 30–40 min on low heat.
2 Chop vegetables and place in pot. Add red wine and simmer until everything is tender. Season to taste if necessary and add sour or double cream just before serving.
Serve with brown bread, baked potatoes or boiled rice.

**Lamb with Dill**
(serves 6–8)
Preparation time: about 10 min
Cooking time: about 1 hr
Suitable for the freezer

*about 1½kg (3¾lb) shoulder of lamb,*
  *on the bone*
*salt, 1 × 15ml tbsp (1tbsp) black*
  *peppercorns*
*2 bay leaves, 1 sprig of dill*
*25g (1oz) butter or margarine*
*3 × 15ml tbsp (3tbsp) plain flour*
*100–200ml (4–7fl oz) double cream*
*100–200 (4–7fl oz) sour cream*

1 Place meat in a large saucepan and add enough water to just cover the meat. Bring to the boil and skim. Turn the heat down and add salt, peppercorns, bay leaves and stems of dill. Simmer until meat is tender.
2 Remove meat, take it off bones, and slice. Sieve the stock. Melt butter over low heat, add flour, and leave to simmer for a few minutes without getting brown. Gradually add stock and double cream, stirring continuously, and bring to just below boiling. Add sour cream and chopped dill fronds. Season to taste with salt. Pour sauce over meat and leave to heat through properly.

## Left-over Lamb Stew
(serves 4)
Preparation time: about 15 min
Cooking time: 20–25 min
Suitable for the freezer

*Left-over, cooked lamb or mutton*
*2 onions, 1 clove of garlic, oil*
*1 stalk of celery, 3 carrots*
*2–3 leeks*
*300–400ml (½–¾pt) stock*
*soy sauce, salt, pepper*
*300–400g (11–14oz) green beans*
*100–150g (4–5oz) spaghetti or*
  *macaroni*
*3–4 × ml tbsp (3–4tbsp) grated*
  *cheese*
*finely chopped parsley*

1 Brown chopped onions and crushed garlic in 1–2 × 15ml tbsp (1–2tbsp) oil, and add cubes of celery and carrot, thick leek rings and stock. Cover, and leave to simmer for about 15 min.
2 Boil broken spaghetti or macaroni in slightly salted water. Drain.
3 Slice meat into small pieces and place them in pot together with sliced green beans. Season to taste with salt, pepper and soy sauce. Leave to cook for 5–10 min then add cooled spaghetti or macaroni, grated cheese and 2–3 × ml tbsp (2–3tbsp) finely chopped parsley.

*Above: Lamb Goulash. Below: Left-over Lamb Stew.*

# Pea, Bean and Lentil Casseroles

*Pulses are a very important source of protein, and we really should use them more often. With other vegetables, or with meat, they make economical and delicious winter fare.*

### Lentil Casserole with Meatballs

(right)
(serves 6–8)
Preparation time: 20–25 min
Soaking time: 3–4 hr
Cooking time: about 30 min in all
Suitable for the freezer

300–400g (11–14oz) sausagemeat
450g (1lb) lentils, salt, peppercorns
2 large onions, 1 parsnip
4–6 carrots
25g (1oz) butter or margarine
400–500 ml (¾–1pt) stock
1 clove of garlic
1–2 × 5ml tbsp (1–2tbsp) vinegar
4 leeks, 1 egg
3 × 15ml tbsp (3tbsp) breadcrumbs
100ml (4fl oz) double cream
marjoram, thyme, nutmeg

1 Rinse lentils and soak in cold water for 3–4 hr. Boil in soaking water until tender, but not quite ready. Pour off water and sprinkle with 1 × 5ml tsp (1tsp) salt.
2 While lentils are cooking, sauté chopped onions and cubes of parsnip and carrots in butter. Add ½ × 5ml tsp (½tsp) salt, together with 8–10 black peppercorns, 300–400ml

### Chopping onions

*1 Peel onion and slice in two. Slice as shown in picture.*

*2 Still holding onion tightly, place it with flat side down and cut lengthways.*

*3 Then chop across at right angles, with the flat side still down.*

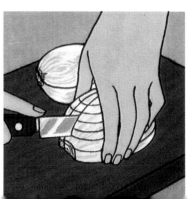

($\frac{1}{2}$–$\frac{3}{4}$pt) stock, crushed garlic, leeks and vinegar. Leave to simmer for about 10–15 min.

3 Mix sausagemeat with egg, breadcrumbs, double cream and about 100ml (4fl oz) stock. The dough must be firm.

Add seasonings and also some dried herbs if you like. Make fairly large meatballs and boil for 6–8 min in slightly salted water.

4 Place lentils in pot with vegetables, together with leek rings and hot meat balls. Leave to simmer on low heat for about 5 min.
Serve with crisp French bread.

## Pea and Ham Casserole
(serves 6–8)
Preparation time: about 30 min
Soaking time: 10–12 hr
Cooking time: about 1–1$\frac{1}{2}$ hr
Suitable for the freezer

*450–700g (1–1$\frac{1}{2}$lb) boiling bacon or ham*
*450g (1lb) dried green peas*
*4 onions, salt, black peppercorns*
*1 slice celeriac or $\frac{1}{2}$ stalk celery*
*1 parsnip*
*2 small leeks, 1 sprig of parsley*
*1 bay leaf, a pinch of dried thyme*

1 Rinse peas and soak in about 1 litre (1$\frac{3}{4}$pt) water for 10–12 hr. Boil in soaking water for about 30–40 min without salting.

2 Add the peeled, chopped vegetables, 6–8 peppercorns, sliced bacon or ham and a bouquet garni of the green part of the leek, celeriac or celery leaves and $\frac{1}{2}$ sprig of parsley, bay leaf and thyme.

3 Leave to simmer until everything is tender, remove bouquet garni and season to taste with salt. Sprinkle with chopped parsley.

NOTE Never add salt to pulses like peas, beans or lentils while they are cooking as this makes them tough. Red kidney beans must *always* be boiled for at least 30 min before eating.

## Beef and Red Kidney Beans
(serves 6–8)
Preparation time: 15–20 min
Soaking time: 10–12 hr (only if using dried beans)
Cooking time: about 1$\frac{1}{2}$ hr
Suitable for the freezer

*700–900g (1$\frac{1}{2}$–2lb) stewing steak*
*350–400g (12–14oz) red kidney beans or 2 × 400g (14oz) cans*

*Above: Two tasty, warming dishes—Pea and Ham Casserole (left) and Beef and Red Kidney Beans (right).*

*3 × 15ml tbsp (3tbsp) oil*
*4 onions, 2 cloves of garlic*
*salt, black pepper, paprika*
*about 1 litre (1$\frac{3}{4}$pt) stock*
*1 can tomato purée*
*1 bay leaf, marjoram, rosemary*
*4–5 × 15ml tbsp (4–5tbsp) sour or double cream*
*3–4 × 15ml tbsp (3–4tbsp) finely chopped chives*

1 Rinse dried beans and soak in cold water for 10–12 hr. Boil in soaking water without salt for 1–1$\frac{1}{2}$ hr, then drain. Drain canned beans well.

2 Chop meat into chunks and brown in oil with chopped onions. Sprinkle with salt, pepper and paprika and add stock and tomato purée, crushed bay leaf and crushed garlic. Add marjoram and rosemary to taste and simmer until meat is tender.

3 Drain the soaked and boiled beans and mix with meat and sauce. Thicken the sauce with flour if you like, and add some sour or double cream. Garnish with chives, and serve with rolls and green salad.

# Haricot Bean Casseroles

*Haricot beans are just as full of protein as the other pulses, and are delicious cold in salads as well as in casseroles.*

### Haricot Bean Casserole
(serves 6–8)
Preparation time: 20–25 min
Soaking time: about 12 hr
Cooking time: about 1½ hr
Suitable for the freezer

*150g (5oz) bacon*
*1 × 15ml tbsp (1tbsp) oil*
*300g (11oz) dried haricot beans*
*3 onions, 4 large carrots*
*2 leeks, 1 sprig of thyme*
*1 sprig of parsley*
*2 × 15ml tbsp (2tbsp) plain flour*
*salt, white peppercorns*

1 Rinse beans and soak in 1 litre (1¾pt) cold water. Boil in the soaking water for about 1 hr without salt.
2 After 1 hr, add 1 × 5ml tsp (1tsp) salt, 6 crushed peppercorns, the quartered onions, carrots in strips, leek rings and a bouquet garni consisting of the green of the leek, thyme and a few sprigs of parsley. Cook on low heat until everything is tender.
3 Brown bacon cubes in oil in another pan, stir in flour and mix in the stock from the beans and vegetables until you get a smooth, not too thick, gravy.
4 Remove bouquet garni, add beans and vegetables to the gravy and season to taste again if needed. Garnish with chopped parsley. Serve with fresh bread.

### TIPS
**Peeling Tomatoes**
Make a small cut in the skin of the tomatoes, then leave them in boiling water for a few minutes. The peel will now come off easily.

*A few vegetables and some bacon scraps add flavour to Haricot Bean Casserole.*

### Polish Bean Casserole (above)
(serves 6–8)
Preparation time: 20–25 min
Soaking time: about 12 hr
Cooking time: about 1½ hr
Suitable for the freezer

*1kg (2¼lb) stewing pork, boned*
*250–300g (9–11oz) dried haricot beans*
*4 leeks, 1 sprig of thyme*
*1 sprig of marjoram, 1 bay leaf*
*1 parsnip*
*2 onions, 1 clove of garlic*
*25–40g (1–1½oz) butter or margarine*
*1 small piece of turnip or swede*
*6–8 carrots, salt, pepper*

1 Rinse beans and soak in 1 litre (1¾pt) cold water for 12 hr. Boil for about 30 min in the soaking water, without salt. Make a bouquet garni of the green part of the leek, thyme, marjoram, and bay leaf and leave to boil with beans.
2 Cut pork shoulder into chunks and sauté in butter with chopped onion and crushed garlic. Sprinkle with salt and pepper. Add meat and onion to the beans, along with sliced carrots, leek rings and cubed turnip or swede and parsnip. Leave to cook until everything is tender, remove bouquet garni, and season to taste with salt and pepper.
Serve with fresh bread.

### Provençal Bean Casserole
(serves 6–8)
Preparation time: 20–25 min
Soaking time: about 12 hr
Cooking time: about 1½ hr
Suitable for the freezer

*450–700g (1–1½lb) lean pork (salted or smoked is nice)*
*250–300g (9–11oz) dried haricot beans*
*2 onions, 4 whole cloves*
*salt, pepper*
*2 cloves of garlic*
*1 bay leaf, a sprig of thyme*
*2 leeks, 1 sprig of parsley*
*½ can peeled tomatoes*
*about 300ml (½pt) red wine*

1 Rinse beans and soak them in about 700ml (1¼pt) cold water for 12 hr. Boil for about 30 min in the soaking water with whole onions spiked with cloves.
2 Add crushed garlic, 2 × 5ml tsp (2tsp) salt, ½ × 5ml tsp (½tsp) ground black pepper and a bouquet garni of bay leaf, thyme, the green part of the leek and ½ sprig of parsley. Add tomatoes, red wine, leek rings and the lean pork cut in cubes. Leave to cook on low heat until everything is tender.
3 Remove bouquet garni and onion with cloves. Season to taste. Sprinkle with chopped parsley and serve with fresh bread rolls.

# Chicken Casseroles

*Chicken is an ideal casserole basic, as the meat is lean and mild in taste, allowing you infinite variation in what you choose to add to flavour it.*

**Luxury Chicken** (above)
(serves 4)
Preparation time: about 20 min
Cooking time: about 30 min
Suitable for the freezer, but the quality will deteriorate.

*1 large chicken or 4–6 chicken legs*
*50g (2oz) butter or margarine*
*plain flour, paprika*
*salt, pepper*
*2 onions, 1 clove of garlic*
*300ml ($\frac{1}{2}$pt) dry white wine*
*1 chicken liver*
*250g (9oz) button mushrooms*
*300ml ($\frac{1}{2}$pt) red wine*
*1 × 15ml tbsp (1tbsp) brandy*
*100ml (4fl oz) double cream*

1 Cut chicken into 4 large or 8 small pieces. Dry them or the legs, and turn in flour seasoned with salt, pepper and paprika.
2 Brown in $\frac{1}{2}$ the butter, with chopped onions and crushed garlic. Pour $\frac{1}{2}$ the white wine over the chicken and bring to the boil. Turn the heat down, and pour the rest of the white wine into the pan. Cover with the lid and simmer gently for about 20 min.
3 Meanwhile melt remaining butter and brown chicken liver and mushrooms. Sprinkle with flour, stir well, and gradually add about $\frac{1}{2}$ the red wine. Stir sauce until smooth and then pour in the rest of the red wine.
4 Put the mushroom sauce into pot with the chicken. Leave to simmer gently on low heat until meat is tender, then stir in brandy and cream. Season to taste.

VARIATION
White wine, red wine and brandy can be replaced by a strong chicken stock with the juice and finely grated rind of 1 lemon.

## Chicken with Tarragon and Cream

(serves 4–6)
Preparation time: 25–30 min
Cooking time: about 30 min
Suitable for the freezer

2 chickens
2 onions
salt, white pepper
40g (1½oz) butter or margarine
¼ litre (9fl oz) double cream
about 200ml (7fl oz) sour cream
2–3 × 15ml tbsp (2–3tbsp) fresh or
   1–2 × 4ml tsp (1–2tsp) dried
   tarragon
2 × 15ml tbsp (2tbsp) chopped
   parsley

1 Joint the chickens into 6–8 pieces each (see illustrations on right). Dry them and rub with salt and pepper. Chop liver, heart, gizzard and neck.
2 Melt butter in a pot and place the chicken pieces in this, along with giblets and chopped onions. Turn pieces in butter and leave to sauté on low heat for 10–15 min. Do not let them go brown.
3 Mix double cream with a little stock, pour over the meat and leave to simmer until the chicken is tender. Place meat on a hot serving dish and leave meat juices to simmer, uncovered. Stir sour cream and tarragon into the gravy and season to taste. Pour over chicken and sprinkle with chopped parsley. Serve with fresh bread rolls and a green salad.

VARIATION
You can also put sliced, lightly sautéed mushrooms into the sauce with the juice of ½ lemon. Add 1–2 egg yolks mixed in sour cream to the sauce (but if you *do* add eggs, do not let the sauce boil again). This should not be frozen.

## Indian Chicken Casserole

(serves 4–6)
Preparation time: 20–25 min
Cooking time: about 30 min
Suitable for the freezer, but the flavour will deteriorate

2 large chickens
2–3 cloves of garlic
salt, pepper, curry powder, ground
   ginger
2 × 15ml tbsp (2tbsp) oil
2 sour apples
about 200ml (7fl oz) yoghurt
2 × 15ml tbsp (2tbsp) desiccated
   coconut
about 200ml (7fl oz) stock
10 shallots or button onions
1 green pepper
a pinch of chilli powder (optional)

1 Joint chickens into about 6–8 pieces each and rub with crushed garlic, 1 × 5ml tsp (1tsp) salt, ¼ × 5ml tsp (¼tsp) pepper and ¼ × 5ml tsp (¼tsp) ground ginger.
2 Brown meat in oil with 1–2 × 5ml tsp (1–2tsp) curry powder, and peeled, cored apples, cut into half-moonshapes. Add yoghurt to pot, put on high heat and shake it or stir mixture carefully to avoid burning.
3 Turn heat down when liquid has nearly evaporated and add coconut, stock, whole onions, finely sliced pepper and a little chilli powder (if used). Cover, and simmer until chicken is tender.
4 Season gravy to taste, and serve straight from the pot with rolls or boiled rice.

## Easy Chicken Fricassée

(serves 4)
Preparation time: about 10 min
Cooking time: about 30 min
Suitable for the freezer without egg yolk and double cream

about ½kg (1lb 2oz) chicken pieces
1 onion, salt, white peppercorns
about 400g (14oz) frozen peas and
   carrots
15g (½oz) butter or margarine
1 × 15ml tbsp (1tbsp) plain flour
100ml (4fl oz) double cream
1 egg yolk
finely chopped parsley

1 Place chicken in a pan with 200–300ml (7–10fl oz) water, onion rings, ½ × 5ml tsp (½tsp) salt and 6–8 peppercorns. Bring to a boil, skim and simmer on low heat with lid on until chicken is tender. Remove chicken and peppercorns. Take meat off bones, and set aside.
2 Boil vegetables for about 5 min in chicken stock. Mix butter and flour and add gradually to the stock to thicken. Add double cream whisked with egg yolk, chopped parsley, and the meat. Season to taste. Leave pot on low heat (do not boil) for a few minutes.

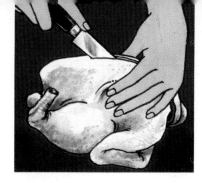

1 Cut chicken in half along the breast bone with a sharp knife.

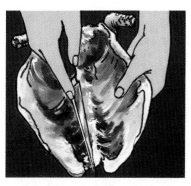

2 Cut along back bone on both sides, so that this can be removed.

3 Cut the half chicken across the middle and/or cut off legs and wings.

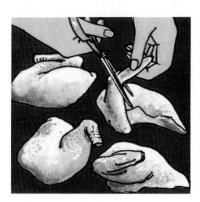

4 Remove wing pinions, and cut leg joints into thigh end drumstick.

Tasty Chicken Curry, here served with small fried potatoes.

2 Simmer on low heat, covered, until chicken is tender. Remove bouquet garni, chicken and onions and sieve stock. Remove the skin and bones, and slice the meat and onions finely.

3 Sauté chopped mushrooms in butter with the curry powder. Add chopped onions, salt, lemon juice and a little finely grated lemon rind. Stir in plain flour, sauté, then dilute with stock and double cream. Leave sauce to simmer for a few minutes, stirring continuously.

4 Place chicken meat in sauce and season to taste with salt, pepper and a dash of crushed, dried sage, and garnish with hard-boiled egg quarters on top.

Serve with small fried potatoes (fry in butter and oil, raw, with a little salt, in a covered pan) or boiled rice (perhaps cooked with chopped onion and a pinch of turmeric).

VARIATION

This curry sauce can be used with left-over cooked poultry. Instead of eggs you can garnish with pepper rings.

## TIPS
### Slicing Eggs

If you are going to use eggs as garnish, either sliced or quartered, use smaller eggs, the yolk and white of which hold together much better.

### Chicken with Mushrooms

(serves 4–6)
Preparation time: 15–20 min
Cooking time: about 30 min
Suitable for the freezer, without mushrooms (which can easily become soft and tough)

2 large chickens
salt, pepper, paprika
200ml (7fl oz) stock and 300ml
(½pt) red wine (or all stock)
100ml (4fl oz) tomato juice
1 × 15ml tbsp (1tbsp) oil
40g (1½oz) butter or margarine,
2 small onions
½kg (1lb 2oz) mushrooms, 1 lemon
2–3 × 5ml tsp (2–3tsp) cornflour
basil

### Chicken Curry

(serves 4–6)
Preparation time: 10–15 min
Cooking time: about 1 hr in all
Suitable for the freezer without the egg

1 large chicken
2–3 onions, 2 celery leaves
1 sprig of thyme, 2 sprigs of parsley
1 bay leaf
25g (1oz) butter or margarine
2–3 × 5ml tsp (2–3tsp) curry powder

250g (9oz) button mushrooms
½ lemon
2 × 15ml tbsp (2tbsp) plain flour,
200ml (7fl oz) double cream, 4 eggs
salt, pepper, sage

1 Place chicken in a pot and add enough water just to cover. Bring to boil and skim. Add 1 × 5ml tsp (1tsp) salt, peeled onions cut in halves, and a bouquet garni made of celery leaves, parsley, thyme and bay leaf.

*A crisp salad goes well with Chicken and Mushrooms.*

1 Joint chickens. Dry meat well and rub with salt, pepper and paprika.
2 Brown chicken and finely chopped onions in oil and 15g (½oz) butter. Turn heat down and add stock and red wine (or just stock) and tomato juice. Leave to simmer, covered, for about 25 min.
3 Slice mushrooms and brown in remaining butter. Season to taste with salt, pepper and lemon juice and pour into pot. Leave to cook for a further 5 min and thicken meat juices with cornflour mixed with cold water. Season to taste again if necessary, and add a little fresh or dried basil.
Serve with boiled rice and a green salad.

### Chicken with Peppers
(serves 4–6)
Preparation time: 15–20 min
Cooking time: about 30 min
Suitable for the freezer, but the peppers will soften

*2 fresh or frozen chickens*
*100g (4oz) bacon*
*25g (1oz) butter or margarine*
*2–3 onions, 400 ml (¾pt) stock*
*salt, pepper, paprika*
*2 red and 1 yellow or green pepper*
*4–6 ripe tomatoes, parsley*

1 Joint chicken. Dry meat and rub with salt, pepper and paprika.
2 Brown small cubes of bacon in pot until golden, add 15g (½oz) butter and brown chopped onions and chicken pieces in the fat. Add stock, cover, and leave to simmer on low heat for about 25 min.
3 Wash and clean peppers and slice finely. Scald and peel tomatoes and cut into quarters. Sauté peppers and tomatoes in remaining butter, and season to taste.
4 Add vegetables to pot with chicken. Leave to simmer for about 5 min and season to taste again if necessary.
Serve with bread, potatoes or boiled rice.

*Chicken with Peppers – a tasty combination.*

# Chicken with Herbs and Spices

*As already said, chicken's mild taste blends beautifully with a large variety of other flavours. Experiment!*

**Chicken with Rosemary**
(below)
(serves 4–6)
Preparation time: about 20 min
Cooking time: about 30 min
Suitable for the freezer, without the mushrooms

2 chickens
salt, pepper, rosemary
2 × 15ml tbsp (2tbsp) oil
200ml (7fl oz) stock
1 × 15ml tbsp (1tbsp) Worcestershire
  sauce
1 × 15ml tbsp (1tbsp) tomato purée
¼l (9 fl oz) double cream

100–225g (¼–½lb) mushrooms
15g (½oz) butter or margarine
lemon juice, 2–3 tomatoes
1 clove of garlic
basil, parsley

1 Joint chickens into four pieces each. Dry meat and rub in a mixture of 1 × 5ml tsp (1tsp) salt, ¼ × 5ml tsp (½tsp) pepper and 1 × 15ml tbsp (1tbsp) fresh or 1 × 5ml tsp (1tsp) dried, rosemary. (The rosemary leaves are like small needles and must be either crushed or chopped very finely.)
2 Brown chicken in oil and add stock, Worcestershire sauce and tomato purée. Simmer on low heat for 20–25 min, with the lid on.
3 Sauté cleaned, chopped mushrooms in butter or margarine and add salt and lemon juice. Pour mushrooms into pot with chicken with double cream, sliced tomatoes, crushed garlic, ½ × 15ml tbsp (½tbsp) fresh or ½ × 5ml tsp (½tsp) dried basil, and 1–2 × 15ml tbsp

(1–2tbsp) chopped parsley.
4 Leave to cook for a further 5–10 min. Add more seasonings and herbs if necessary.
Serve with Garlic bread.
5 Make cuts in a French loaf at 3–4cm (1½in) intervals, but do not slice right through. Mix soft butter with crushed garlic, chopped parsley, lemon juice, salt and white pepper. Spread butter into the cuts and place loaf in oven for about 6–8 min at 240°3, 475°K, Gas 9.

**Chicken with Onions**
(serves 4–6)
Preparation time: 20–25 min
Cooking time: about 30 min
Suitable for the freezer

2 chickens
1 × 15ml tbsp (1tbsp) oil
25g (1oz) butter or margarine
salt, pepper, paprika
1 × 5ml tsp (1tsp) dried mixed herbs
200–300ml (7–10fl oz) stock and
  150ml (¼pt) white wine (or all

stock)
*4 ripe tomatoes*
*1–2 cloves of garlic*
*1 × 15ml tbsp (1tbsp) plain flour*
*200ml (7fl oz) sour or double cream*
*about 75g (3oz) pickling or pickled
  onions*
*chopped parsley*

1 Joint chickens. Dry well and brown in oil with ½ the butter or margarine. Sprinkle with salt, pepper, paprika and mixed herbs.
2 Add stock and white wine (or stock only), peeled, sliced tomatoes and crushed garlic, and leave to simmer for 20–25 min with lid on. If using pickling onions, peel and cook for last 10 min.
3 Remove chicken pieces from pot and pick away all bones. Whisk a mixture of remaining soft butter or margarine and flour into meat juices. Leave to cook for a few minutes, then add sour or double cream, well drained pickled onions, 1–2 × 15ml tbsp (1–2tbsp) chopped parsley and the meat. Season to taste. Heat dish thoroughly, but carefully, not letting it boil!
Serve with French bread and a green salad.

## Chicken with Lemon

(serves 4–6)
Preparation time: about 20 min
Cooking time: about 45 min
Suitable for the freezer

*2 chickens*
*1 onion, 2 leeks*
*1 slice of celeriac or 1 stalk of celery*
*salt, white peppercorns, 2 lemons*
*15g (½oz) butter or margarine*
*1 × 15ml tbsp (1tbsp) plain flour*
*100ml (4fl oz) double cream, lemon
  balm*
*parsley, cress or watercress to garnish*

1 Place chickens in a large pot and add water until nearly covered. Bring to boil and skim.
2 Add 1 × 5ml tsp (1tsp) salt, 6–8 peppercorns, chopped onion, leek rings and grated celeriac or finely chopped celery. Wash lemons well, place slices of 1 lemon only in pot and simmer, covered, until vegetables are tender. Remove vegetables, and cook until chicken is tender.
3 Make a sauce of butter or margarine, plain flour and about ¼ litre (9 fl oz) sieved stock. Slice thin, even

slices from ½ remaining lemon and squeeze the juice from the end parts into the gravy. Bring to boil, turn heat down, and add double cream. Stir well, and season to taste with 3–4 × 15ml tbsp (3–4tbsp) chopped lemon balm, salt and pepper.
4 Remove skin and bones from chickens and heat meat in sauce. Garnish with slices from remaining lemon half and sprinkle with finely chopped parsley, cress or watercress.

## Chicken Casserole with Rice

(serves 4)
Preparation time: 15–20 min
Cooking time: about 40 min
Suitable for the freezer, but will lose some flavour

*1 large chicken*
*plain flour, salt, pepper, curry
  powder*
*40g (1½oz) butter or margarine*
*225g (8oz) long-grain rice*
*1 onion, saffron or turmeric*
*500–600ml (about 1pt) stock*
*1 large can tomatoes*
*10 stuffed olives or 2 × 15ml tbsp
  (2tbsp) capers*
*1 sprig of parsley*

*Above: Chicken with Onions.*

1 Joint chicken into 8 pieces, dry them and turn in 3–4 × 15ml tbsp (3–4tbsp) plain flour mixed with ½ × 5ml tsp (½tsp) salt, ¼ × 5ml tsp (¼tsp) pepper and ½ × 5ml tsp (½tsp) curry powder.
2 Brown chicken pieces in a frying pan in 25g (1oz) butter or margarine on medium heat. Turn heat down, sprinkle with salt, put a lid on and leave meat to cook for about 20 min.
3 Sauté finely chopped onion in a pot in remaining butter or margarine. Add rice, the majority of the stock, ½–1 × 5ml tsp (½–1tsp) salt and pinch of saffron or ½ × 5ml tsp (½tsp) turmeric. Stir, cover, and cook on low heat for about 20 min.
4 Place whole, well rinsed tomatoes in the pot with chicken, and leave to heat through (5–10 min).
5 Stir rice with a fork and add sliced olives or capers, and a little stock if the rice appears too dry. Place rice on a hot serving dish and arrange the chicken and tomatoes on top. Garnish with fresh parsley.
Serve hot with bread, butter and a green salad.

# The Chinese way

## Peking Casserole
(serves 4–6)
Preparation time: 15–20 min
Marination time: 2 hr
Cooking time: 10–15 min
Can be frozen but will lose flavour

700g (1½lb) fillet of pork (or other
   lean cut)
4 × 15ml tbsp (4tbsp) sherry
4 × 15ml tbsp (4tbsp) soy sauce
1 × 5ml tsp (1tsp) brown sugar
1 × 5ml tsp (1tsp) ground ginger
4 cloves of garlic
4 × 15ml tbsp (4tbsp) oil
3 large onions, 2–3 peppers
4–6 tomatoes
200–300ml (7–10fl oz) stock
1 × 5ml tsp (1tsp) cornflour
salt, pepper

1 Cut meat in thin slices and leave
for 2 hr in a marinade of sherry, soy
sauce, ½ the oil, brown sugar, ginger
and 2 crushed cloves of garlic.
2 Pat meat dry and brown with
onion rings in remaining oil. Add
remaining crushed garlic, sliced
peppers, peeled chopped tomatoes,
stock and some of the marinade.
3 Leave casserole to simmer until
meat is tender, but the vegetables
should still be crisp. Season to taste
with marinade, salt and pepper, and
thicken the gravy with cornflour
mixed in a little cold water.

## Sweet and Sour Pork Casserole
(serves 4–6)
Preparation time: 20–25 min
Marination time: 1 hr
Cooking time: 30–40 min
Suitable for the freezer, but will
deteriorate in quality and taste

450–700g (1–1½lb) lean boneless
   pork
2 × 15ml tbsp (2tbsp) vinegar
3 × 15ml tbsp (3tbsp) soy sauce
4 × 15ml tbsp (4tbsp) oil
400ml (¾pt) stock
2 peppers, 2 leeks
10–12 shallots or small onions
¼ cucumber, 3 carrots
250g (9oz) mushrooms
salt, pepper
1–2 × 5ml tsp (1–2tsp) honey
2 × 5ml tsp (2tsp) cornflour

1 Cut meat into cubes and place in a
dish. Cover with marinade of vinegar, soy sauce, ½ the oil and 100ml
(4fl oz) stock. Cover dish and place
in a cool place.
2 Dry meat and brown slightly in
remaining oil. Sprinkle with salt and
pepper, pour remaining stock over
and bring to boil with the lid on.
3 Finely chop onions and vegetables, place in pot, bring back to the
boil, and cook until vegetables are
nearly ready, but still crisp.
4 Season meat juices to taste with
marinade, the honey, and salt and
pepper if necessary. Thicken with
cornflour mixed with cold water.

## Quick Chinese Casserole
(serves 4)
Preparation time: 15–20 min
Cooking time: 10 min in all
Not suitable for the freezer

450g (1lb) lean pork (fillet)
2–3 × 15ml tbsp (2–3tbsp) oil
salt, pepper, paprika
2 carrots
¼ white cabbage (about 450g or 1lb)
4 thin leeks, 250g (9oz) mushrooms
4 stalks of celery
250g (9oz) beansprouts
white cabbage
50ml (2fl oz) dry sherry
soy sauce

1 Slice meat thinly. Wash and prepare the vegetables and cut into thin
slices or shreds.
2 Heat 1–2 × 15ml tbsp (1–2tbsp)
oil in a wide frying pan (or a wok,
which is absolutely right for this
recipe). Brown meat, stirring all the
time, and season. When brown,
push meat to the side of the pan.
3 Add vegetables in the order in
which they are listed above, so
that, for instance the carrots have
6–8 min cooking time, and the
cabbage 1 min. Mix carefully with
the pork. Season to taste with soy
sauce, sherry and more seasoning.

*Below: Sweet and Sour Pork
Casserole. Right: Peking Casserole.*

Vegetable and Pork Casserole – a meal in itself.

*1–1½kg (2¼–3¼lb) lightly salted belly of pork*
*2 onions, 6 carrots*
*6–8 potatoes, 4 leeks*
*celery leaves*
*1kg (2¼lb) fresh or 1 packet frozen peas*
*salt, pepper, parsley*

1 Place pork in a pot with about 1 litre (1¾pt) water, bring to boil and skim. Cover, and simmer for 1 hr.
2 Add sliced onions, leeks, carrots and potatoes, as well as a bouquet garni made of the green of the leek, the celery leaves, and ½ sprig of parsley. Simmer for 15 min longer.
3 Place fresh or frozen peas in the pot. Remove pork and season stock to taste with salt and freshly ground pepper. Continue cooking until vegetables are tender. Cut pork in slices and place back in pot.
Garnish with finely chopped parsley and serve with brown bread, French bread or crispbread.

## Mustard Pork with Brussels Sprouts
(serves 6–8)
Preparation time: about 20 min
Cooking time about 40 min
Suitable for the freezer

*about 1½kg (3¼lb) smoked pork or lean pork*
*2 onions, 1 parsnip*
*½ celeriac or 4 stalks celery*
*25g (1oz) butter or margarine*
*1 × 4ml tsp (1tsp) curry powder*
*1kg (2¼lb) small potatoes*
*½kg (about 1lb) Brussels sprouts*
*1 × 15ml tbsp (1tbsp) plain flour*
*dry mustard*
*200ml (7fl oz) single or double cream*
*salt, pepper, cress*

1 Chop up the onions and cut meat into large cubes. Cut celeriac or celery and parsnip into small cubes.
2 Sauté lightly in ½ the butter or margarine with curry powder, and add small peeled potatoes. Add water to barely cover contents and simmer with lid on for about 30 min. Place whole, cleaned Brussels sprouts in casserole and boil for another 10 min.
3 Mix remaining soft butter or mar-

# Lunch or Supper Casseroles

*The following recipes are pork casseroles, all simple and tasty. If you can find smoked pork, it is delicious, adding a wonderful smoky flavour, as does the salted belly.*

## Autumn Casserole
(serves 6–8)
Preparation time: about 30 min
Cooking time: 40–50 min
Suitable for the freezer, but do not boil when re-heating

*1½kg (3¼lb) lightly salted belly of pork*
*about 100g (4oz) garlic sausage*
*1 white cabbage, 1–2 cloves of garlic*
*2–3 onions, 4–6 carrots*
*4 leeks, 2 bay leaves*
*salt, black peppercorns, parsley*
*2 egg yolks*
*200ml (7fl oz) double cream*

1 Chop cabbage in fairly large chunks, mix with crushed garlic and place in a large pot or casserole.
2 Slice pork and place in layers in pot with onion rings, carrot slices, sausage slices and leek rings. Place bay leaves on top, sprinkle with a pinch of salt and 10–12 peppercorns.
3 Add enough water to barely cover contents and simmer with lid on until meat is tender. Add more water if necessary. Do not allow to boil dry.
4 Pour stock (about 300ml or ½pt) into another pot and add cream whisked with egg yolks. Stir well and let gravy boil gently until it reaches the right consistency. Season to taste with salt, pepper and parsley. Pour gravy into casserole. Serve with brown bread.

## Vegetable and Pork Casserole
(serves 6–8)
Preparation time: about 30 min
Cooking time: about 1½ hr
Suitable for the freezer

*A casserole made up with a packeted soup.*

garine with plain flour and 2–3 × 5ml tsp (23tsp) dry mustard. Stir this into meat juices. Cook and stir until gravy is smooth, then stir in double cream and season to taste with salt, pepper and more mustard. Sprinkle with chopped cress, and serve with French bread.

### TIPS

For Busy Cooks
Never feel ashamed of making things easier for yourself. The shops have a wide selection of semi-prepared foodstuffs available – packaged soups, canned soups, lots of frozen goods – and these make a good basis for a casserole. By adding vegetables, potatoes, meat and/or sausages with a touch of spices, you can give your own special touch to the finished dish.
In addition there are also basic sauce mixes, in cans or packets, which you add to chicken or meat. Many of these are quite tasty, but don't hesitate to add more spices or vegetables if you feel like it. Accompany them with boiled potatoes or rice.

### Pork Casserole with Peas
(serves 6–8)
Preparation time: about 20 min
Cooking time: about 1 hr
Suitable for the freezer

*1–1½kg (2¼–3¼lb) smoked pork or*
  *lean pork*
*100g (4oz) bacon*
*½ celeriac or 4 stalks of celery*
*6 carrots, 1 parsnip*
*4 leeks, 1 bay leaf*
*1 sprig of thyme, 1 kg (2¼lb) fresh or*
  *1 packet frozen peas*
*15g (½oz) butter or margarine,*
*1½ × 15ml tbsp (1½tbsp) plain flour*
*salt, pepper, parsley*

1 Cut bacon into small cubes and brown slightly in large pot.
2 Scrape all vegetables and slice. Place celeriac or celery, carrots and parsnip in the bacon fat, add about 1 litre (1¾pt) water and a bouquet garni made of parsley, the green part of the leek, bay leaf and thyme.
3 Simmer for 25–30 min with the lid on. Add leek rings, and cubes of pork. Boil until meat is tender, adding peas about 10 min before end of cooking time.
4 Remove bouquet garni. Mix butter and flour together, stir into meat juices, and boil and stir until gravy is smooth. Season to taste with salt, pepper and plenty of finely chopped parsley.
Serve hot with boiled potatoes.

VARIATION
This recipe can be made both simpler and cheaper and still be as tasty. Start by making up a packet of pea soup. Add vegetables according to taste and time of the year. Heat smoked sausages cut into cubes in the pot for the last few minutes. Sprinkle with crisp slices of bacon or croutons just before serving.

Pork and Turnip Casserole is both tasty and filling.

¼ celeriac or 2 stalks of celery
paprika
300–400ml (½–¾pt) stock
150ml (¼pt) red wine
1 small can tomato purée
chervil, marjoram, basil
1 × 15ml tbsp (1tbsp) plain flour
3 × 15ml tbsp (3tbsp) plain yoghurt

1 Fry small bacon cubes until golden in half the butter in a casserole. Slice meat into fairly large chunks and fry also. Turn heat to low. Wash and peel vegetables.
2 Chop onions and cut turnips, potatoes and celeriac or celery into cubes. Put everything into casserole. Sauté for about 10 min. Sprinkle with salt, pepper and paprika.
3 Add stock, red wine and tomato purée along with 1 × 15ml tbsp (1tbsp) finely chopped chervil, a little fresh or dried marjoram and basil. Put lid on and leave to simmer for 40–50 min until meat is tender.
4 Thicken stock with flour and yoghurt mixed together. You can also add a further 1–2 × 5ml tsp (1–2tsp) paprika.
Serve with fresh bread or rice.

### Winter Casserole
(serves 6–8)
Preparation time: about 30 min
Cooking time: about 1 hr
Suitable for the freezer

700–900g (1½–2lb) stewing pork
  (shoulder cut)
2 onions
25–40g (1–1½oz) butter or
  margarine
salt, pepper
4 carrots, 1 kohlrabi or swede
1 parsnip, 3–4 leeks
¼ celeriac or 2 stalks of celery
½ litre (about 1pt) stock
parsley, chervil

1 Slice meat into chunks and brown in butter in casserole with chopped onions. Wash, peel and slice everything except the leeks into cubes. Place in pot with meat.
2 Sprinkle with salt and pepper, and stock and leave to cook under the lid on low heat until nearly tender. Add leek rings and leave to cook for a further 10 min.
3 Season to taste with salt and

# Pork and Winter Vegetables

*All kinds of root vegetables mix deliciously with fresh or leftover pork in casseroles. And you can use sausages to have an even more reasonable, but just as tasty, meal.*

**Pork and Turnip Casserole**
(serves 6–8)
Preparation time: 20–25 min
Cooking time: about 1 hr
Suitable for the freezer

1kg (2¼lb) stewing pork (shoulder or
  blade)
50g (2oz) bacon
25g (1oz) butter or margarine
3–4 onions
2 small turnips, 6–8 potatoes
salt, pepper

pepper and sprinkle with finely chopped parsley or chervil.

Serve piping hot with fresh bread or boiled potatoes garnished with chopped parsley.

## Kohlrabi or Swede Casserole
(above)
(serves 6–8)
Preparation time: about 20 min
Cooking time: $1-1\frac{1}{2}$ hr
Suitable for the freezer

*1kg ( 2¼lb ) lightly salted pork*
*1 kohlrabi or 2 small swedes*
*8 potatoes, 2 carrots, 2 onions*
*2 bay leaves, 1 sprig of thyme*
*salt, black peppercorns*
*parsley, butter*

1 Place meat in a casserole and add enough water to barely cover. Bring to the boil and skim well.

2 Wash and prepare vegetables, slice them and place in casserole with bay leaves, thyme and 8–10 peppercorns.

3 Place lid on casserole and bring to boil on low heat. Simmer until meat is tender, remove meat and slice. Remove bay leaves and thyme.

4 Stir vegetables vigorously until they break up, or you can mash them if you like. Stir a knob of butter into the vegetable mash, place meat slices into the mash and sprinkle with chopped parsley.

Serve hot with brown bread and strong mustard.

## Ham and Chinese Cabbage

(serves 4)
Preparation time: about 15 min
Cooking time: 20–30 min
Suitable for the freezer, but flavour will deteriorate

300–400g (11–14oz) cooked ham or
 gammon
1–2 Chinese cabbages, 2 small leeks
25g (1oz) butter or margarine
salt, pepper
about 300g (11oz) cooked green
 beans
6–8 small tomatoes
200ml (7fl oz) stock
1 sprig of parsley

1 Clean leeks, slice in rings and sauté in butter for about 5 min on low heat.
2 Rinse cabbage thoroughly, shake off excess water. Slice in narrow strips, crosswise, and place in casserole in layers with strips of ham, leek, sliced beans and halved tomatoes.
3 Sprinkle salt and pepper in between layers, pour stock over and leave to simmer under lid for 15–20 min. Finely chop parsley and stir carefully into casserole.
Serve hot with fresh bread or boiled potatoes.

## Cauliflower Casserole

(serves 4)
Preparation time: about 20 min
Cooking time: about 40 min
Not suitable for the freezer

300–400g (11–14oz) gammon or
 smoked pork
2 onions, 2 whole cloves
4 leeks, 1 cauliflower
100–175g (4–6oz) frozen peas
salt, pepper
25g (1oz) butter or margarine
1½ × 15ml tbsp (1½ tbsp) plain flour
250ml (9fl oz) double cream
mild grated cheese

1 Cut away any bone or gristle from the meat. Place in a pan with enough water to barely cover. Add cleaned onions spiked with cloves. Leave to simmer on low heat until meat is just tender (it will go dry if you cook it too long).
2 Slice leek in rings, divide cauliflower into flowerets. Remove meat and cloves from onions. Cook all vegetables for about 10 min in the

stock, and then remove from stock. Keep warm.
3 Melt butter, stir in flour and gradually add stock and cream, stirring until smooth. Leave to simmer for about 5 min. Remove casserole from the heat and stir about 100g (4oz) grated cheese into sauce. Stir until cheese has melted and season to taste with salt and white pepper.
4 Slice meat and add to sauce with the vegetables. As a variation you can sprinkle more cheese on dish and brown in the oven or under the grill.
Serve with fresh bread rolls and a green salad.

## Pork with Brussels Sprouts

(below)
(serves 6–8)
Preparation time: 15–20 min
Cooking time: about 1 hr
Suitable for the freezer

1½kg (3¼lb) pork shoulder (boned)
4 onions
50g (2oz) butter or margarine
salt, pepper, paprika
½ litre (about 1pt) stock
parsley, thyme, sage
6–8 potatoes
450g (1lb) Brussels sprouts
about 200ml (7fl oz) sour or double
 cream

1 Slice onion into rings and meat into cubes and fry in butter. Add salt and pepper, stock, 1 × 15ml tbsp (1tbsp) chopped parsley and ½ × 15ml tbsp (½tbsp) fresh or ½ × 5ml tsp (½tsp) dried thyme and sage.
2 Cover, and simmer for about 30 min. Peel potatoes, slice, and cook with meat for about 10–15 min. Clean Brussels sprouts, cut off stems and rinse in cold water. Place sprouts in casserole and cook until everything is tender. Season to taste with more salt if necessary.
3 Place sour or whipped cream in blobs on top or stir into gravy. Sprinkle with paprika and serve hot with brown bread.

## Pork Goulash (right)

(serves 6–8)
Preparation time: about 20 min
Cooking time: 40–50 min
Suitable for the freezer

1kg (2¼lb) lean pork (tenderloin or
 boned shoulder)
2 large onions
40g (1½oz) butter or margarine
¼ white cabbage
paprika, salt, pepper
400–500 ml (¾–1pt) stock
2 × 15ml tbsp (2tbsp) tomato purée
½ × 15ml tbsp (½tbsp) soy sauce

2 bay leaves, 1 sprig of thyme
½ sprig of parsley, 4 tomatoes
2 small pickled gherkins
1 red pepper, cornflour
vinegar

1 Slice pork, and cut slices into strips. Peel onion, cut into rings and cook meat and onion in butter, in stages. Do not cook too much meat at one time as it will 'stew' rather than sauté. Season with salt, pepper and paprika, and place batches in casserole as you go along.
2 Shred cabbage and sauté in frying pan for about 10 min until lightly golden. Put in casserole. Deglaze the pan with stock, tomato purée and soy sauce and pour into the casserole. Add a bouquet garni of the herbs. Cover and leave to cook for about 20–25 min.
3 Peel and quarter tomatoes, and add to casserole together with pickled gherkin slices and finely shredded pepper. Leave to simmer until everything is tender and thicken meat juices with 1–2 × 5ml tsp (1–2tsp) cornflour mixed with cold water. Add a few drops of vinegar and more seasoning if necessary. Serve hot with buttered noodles.

## Spring Cabbage Casserole
(serves 6–8)
Preparation time: about 20 min
Cooking time: 1–1½hr
Suitable for the freezer

1–1½kg (2½–3¾lb) pork shoulder (boned)
25g (1oz) butter or margarine
salt, pepper, nutmeg
3 large onions
1 spring cabbage
450g (1lb) carrots
175–225g (6–8oz) frozen peas
400ml (¾pt) stock
1 sprig of parsley
finely chopped chives

1 Cut meat into cubes and sauté in butter on low heat. Sprinkle with salt and pepper, add stock and leave to simmer, covered, for about 45–60 min until meat is nearly ready.
2 Meanwhile scrape and peel vegetables. Cut onions into quarters and shred cabbage. Slice carrots lengthways and then into strips.
3 Put onion, cabbage and carrots into the casserole for about 10–15 min. The peas, finely chopped chives and parsley should be added for the last 4–5 min. Season to taste with more salt and some grated nutmeg.

## TIPS
A small pinch of salt will stop fat spitting out of the frying pan.
Sprinkle a dirty frying pan with ordinary cooking salt and wipe clean with paper kitchen towels – and your pan will be sparkling clean.

into colander and rinse with cold water. Leave to drain. If using mince or sausagemeat, shape into balls, and sauté gently until brown in some extra butter.

2 Chop leeks, clean and slice beans, and steam vegetables in butter on low heat for about 5 min. Add 300ml (½pt) water or stock, salt and pepper and bring to the boil.

3 Heat meatballs in casserole. Whip cream and egg yolk with a little of the boiling stock. Pour back into pot and stir carefully until sauce starts to boil. Take casserole off the heat, and add herbs, cheese, more seasonings, and freshly grated nutmeg to taste.

## Moussaka (right)
(serves 6–8)
Preparation time: 20–25 min
Cooking time: about 1 hr
Oven temperature: 200°C, 400°F, Gas 6
Suitable for the freezer

*700g (1½lb) roughly minced lamb*
*1kg (2¼lb) potatoes*
*300–400g (11–14oz) aubergine or*
  *courgettes*
*salt, pepper, paprika*
*3 slices of crustless white bread*
*1 large can of tomatoes*
*2 onions, marjoram, basil*
*about 300ml (½pt) double cream*
*chives, grated cheese*

1 Slice potatoes thinly. Wash the courgettes or aubergine, slice and place in a colander sprinkled with coarse salt. If the skins are tough, peel them first.

2 Place crumbled bread in a bowl, add tomatoes and minced lamb, grated or finely chopped onion, salt, pepper and paprika, and 1 × 15ml tbsp (1tbsp) marjoram and basil. Mix together well.

3 Pour 3–4 × 15ml tbsp (3–4tbsp) double cream into a large greased casserole and place one layer of potato slices on top. Sprinkle with spices and a thin layer of grated cheese. Place courgette or aubergine slices, meat and potatoes in layers, finishing off with potato slices and sprinkle them with grated cheese.

4 Place lid on casserole and put in preheated oven. Remove lid for the last 10 min to allow surface to become golden. Sprinkle with finely chopped chives and serve casserole with a green salad and bread.

# Minced Meat Casseroles

**Spicy Shepherd's Pie** (above)
(serves 6–8)
Preparation time: about 20 min
Cooking time: about 35 min
Oven temperature: 220°C, 425°F, Gas 7
Suitable for the freezer

*700g (1½lb) beef mince*
*1kg (2¼lb) potatoes*
*3 onions*
*40–50g (1½–2oz) butter or*
  *margarine*
*salt, pepper, 100ml (4fl oz) stock*
*grated fresh horseradish or*
  *horseradish cream sauce*
*1 egg + 1 egg yolk*
*50–100g (2–4oz) bacon slices*
*50g (2oz) grated cheese*

1 Boil peeled, sliced potatoes in unsalted water. Drain well, then mash and whip in 15–25g (½–1oz) butter or margarine, salt, pepper and horseradish. Cool and chill.

2 Sauté 2 chopped onions in 15g (½oz) butter or margarine, add the mince, and brown the lot, stirring continuously. Add stock and season to taste. Cook for about 20 min.

3 Whisk egg and egg yolk into some of the chilled potato mash and place mashed potatoes and mince in layers in a greased ovenproof dish. The top layer should be mashed potatoes.

4 Sprinkle onion rings from remaining onion, small shreds of bacon and grated cheese on top. Add a few knobs of butter and place dish in oven until piping hot and golden.

**Green Spaghetti Casserole**
(serves 4)
Preparation time: 10–15 min
Cooking time: 10–15 min
Not suitable for the freezer

*about 300g (11oz) meat balls (made*
  *from beef mince, pork*
  *sausagemeat, or from a can)*
*200g (7oz) spaghetti*
*250g (9oz) green beans, 4 leeks*
*15g (½oz) butter or margarine*
*100–175g (4–6oz) frozen peas*
*1 egg yolk*
*100ml (4fl oz) double cream*
*mixed herbs*
*grated cheese, salt, pepper, nutmeg*

1 Break spaghetti into bits and boil for 3–4 min *less* than usual, or than indicated on packet. Pour spaghetti

# Rice and Grain Casseroles

*Rice and grains like barley millet and corn are all marvellous sources of energy and fibre. They are economical, filling and tasty.*

## Brown Rice Casserole

(serves 4)
Preparation time: about 15 min
Cooking time: 30–40 min
Suitable for the freezer

*about 300g (11oz) lean stewing*
*    steak (chuck)*
*2 large onions*
*2 × 15ml tbsp (2tbsp) oil*
*salt, pepper, paprika*
*250g (9oz) brown rice*
*1 large can of tomatoes*
*1 × 15ml tbsp (1tbsp) soy sauce*
*about 1 litre (1¾pt) stock*
*2 small pickled gherkins*
*1 bunch of chives*
*1 × 5ml tsp (1tsp) cornflour (if*
*    necessary)*

1 Cut meat in strips and brown in oil with chopped onions.

2 Turn down heat, sprinkle with salt, pepper and paprika, and stir in rice and tomatoes. Add soy sauce and about 700ml (1¼pt) hot stock, and leave to simmer for about 20 min under a lid.

3 Add more stock if the rice looks as though it will boil dry. Add small gherkin cubes and cook until everything is tender. If there is any stock left in the casserole, thicken it with cornflour mixed in a little cold water. Season to taste and add chopped chives.

## Barley Casserole

(serves 6–8)
Preparation time: about 20 mn
Soaking time: 12 hr
Cooking time: 1–1½ hr
Suitable for the freezer

*about 1½kg (3¼lb) stewing beef*
*    (chuck)*
*200g (7oz) barley*
*25g (1oz) butter or margarine*
*2 onions*
*6 carrots, 4–6 potatoes*
*6 large leeks*
*salt, pepper*
*fresh or dried thyme*
*1 bay leaf*
*celery leaves*

Be sure to get some beef bones from the butcher when you buy your meat.

1 Rinse barley and soak in cold water for 12 hr.

2 Cut meat in cubes and brown in butter. Add chopped onions and thick carrot slices, and sauté with meat.

3 Place the beef bones in a large pot along with a bouquet garni made of top of leeks, bay leaf and the celery leaves. Sprinkle with salt, pepper and ½ × 15ml tbsp (½tbsp) finely chopped fresh or ½ × 5ml tsp (½tsp) dried thyme, and add water or stock to barely cover.

4 Add soaked barley and peeled potato cubes and simmer for about 1 hr. Add leek rings. Remove bouquet garni and bones, season to taste, and leave casserole to cook until everything is tender.
Serve warm with brown bread.

*Barley Casserole is filling and very tasty. This recipe contains beef and winter vegetables.*

*Italian Rice Casserole with olives, courgettes and pepper.*

## Corn and Ham Casserole
(serves 4)
Preparation time: about 10 min
Cooking time: about 10 min
Suitable for the freezer

*100–200g (4–7oz) cooked ham or
    gammon
4 leeks
25g (1oz) butter or margarine
300–400g (11–14oz) sweetcorn
    (frozen or canned)
300–400ml (½–¾pt) stock
1–2 × 5ml tsp (1–2tsp) mustard
50–100g (2–4oz) cream cheese
100–200ml (4–7fl oz) double cream
salt, pepper
finely chopped parsley*

1 Cut cleaned leeks into rings and steam for a couple of minutes in butter. Add sweetcorn, ham cubes, stock and mustard and simmer for about 5 min.
2 Mash cream cheese and whisk or stir it smooth with double cream. Stir into casserole and season to taste with salt and pepper. Sprinkle with chopped parsley.
Serve with bread and a salad.

## Italian Rice Casserole
(serves 6–8)
Preparation time: about 15 min
Cooking time: about 1 hr

*about 700g (1½lb) good stewing veal
2 × 15ml tbsp (2tbsp) oil, 2 onions
salt, pepper, rosemary
about 1½ litre (about 2½pt) stock
250g (9oz) long-grain rice
1 yellow (or red) and 1 green pepper
1 large courgette or ½ cucumber
15g (½oz) butter or margarine
15–20 stuffed olives*

1 Cut meat into small chunks and brown them slightly in oil with chopped onions. Sprinkle with salt, pepper and about ½ × 5ml tsp (½tsp) dried, crushed rosemary, and add the stock. Cover and simmer for about 30 min.
2 Add rice and cleaned, sliced peppers and cook for a further 15–20 min. Wash the courgette or cucumber, slice and sauté in melted butter without browning. Place slices in casserole with halved olives and leave to simmer for a few min-utes. Season to taste. Add more stock if necessary.
Serve with bread and tomato salad.

## Millet Casserole with Meatballs
(serves 4)
Preparation time: about 15 min
Cooking time: about 10 min
Suitable for the freezer, but might lose some taste

*1 large can meatballs
225g (8oz) millet grains
¾–1 litre (about 1¼–1¾pt) stock
250g (9oz) green beans
450g (1lb) fresh or frozen peas
2 chicory heads or 1 Chinese cabbage
salt, pepper
1 sprig of parsley*

1 Rinse the millet grains in cold water (you can buy millet in health-food shops). Drain well.
2 Pour millet into boiling stock and stir. Add sliced green beans and sliced chicory or cabbage, and cook for 8–10 min.
3 Add peas, meatballs and lots of chopped parsley. Leave everything to cook for a couple of minutes and season to taste with spices.
Serve hot with bread and mustard.

57

# Vegetables all Year Round

*Vegetables are tasty and good for you, and can be used in casseroles all the year round.*

## Cucumber Casserole

(serves 4)
Preparation time: 15–20 min
Draining time: 1–2 hr
Cooking time: about 15 min
Not suitable for the freezer

*about 450g (1lb) lean pork
(shoulder or tenderloin)
1 large cucumber, 2 onions
1 × 15ml tbsp (1tbsp) coarse salt
25g (1oz) butter or margarine*

*4 tomatoes
300ml (½pt) stock
100ml (4fl oz) double cream
2 egg yolks
dill, basil, pepper*

1 Peel and cut cucumber in half lengthways. Remove seeds and slice it into 5cm (2in) strips. Sprinkle with salt and leave for about 1–2 hr (this draining or 'dégorging' takes liquid out of the vegetable, and strong flavours). Drain well.
2 Slice meat, bash it lightly and cut in thin strips. Sauté along with chopped onions in butter.
3 Scald and peel tomatoes, cut in four and add to meat and onions in casserole with stock and drained cucumber strips.
4 Simmer casserole for 12–15 min. Stir in egg yolks, whisked with cream. Do *not* bring back to boil! Season to taste.
Serve with boiled potatoes.

## Belgian Winter Casserole

(serves 6–8)
Preparation time: about 20 min
Cooking time: about 1½ hr
Suitable for the freezer

*1–1½kg (2¼–3¼lb) lightly salted beef
(brisket)
2 onions, 5 carrots
salt, pepper
¼ celeriac or 2 stalks of celery
1 red pepper
2 leeks, 1 bunch of chives
175g (6oz) boiled rice
450g (1lb) fresh or frozen peas*

1 Bring meat to boil with about 2 litre (3½pt) water, and skim well. Put peeled onions, carrots and celeriac or celery into pot and cook until they are tender. Remove vegetables and cut in cubes. Sieve the stock.
2 Simmer cleaned, chopped pepper and leek rings until tender in meat stock and add chopped meat, boiled vegetables, rice, peas and spices. Sprinkle with chopped chives when the casserole is thoroughly heated. Serve with toasted brown bread.

*Cucumber is an unusual ingredient in this casserole.*

## Carrot Casserole

(serves 4)
Preparation time: 15–20 min
Cooking time: about 15 min
Suitable for the freezer, but might
deteriorate in flavour

*150–200g (5–7oz) bacon or*
  *gammon, 2 onions*
*8 carrots, 300–400ml (½–¾pt) stock*
*250g (9oz) mushrooms*
*25g (1oz) butter or margarine*
*1 lemon, salt, pepper, parsley*

1 Chop bacon or gammon into thin
strips, brown lightly in a casserole
and drain on absorbent paper.
2 Sauté chopped onions and thin
carrot slices in bacon fat for about
5 min on low heat. Add stock and
simmer for about 5 min.
3 Sauté cleaned, chopped mushrooms in the butter and add salt,
pepper and lemon juice. Mix mushrooms and bacon with onions and
carrots in casserole, reheat, and
season to taste with spices and finely
chopped parsley.
Serve with bread or potatoes.

*Belgian Winter Casserole – a delicious version of the soup casserole.*

*Carrot Casserole is cheap and tasty.*

59

# Sausages

*There are many different types of sausages used in these recipes. You don't have to necessarily use the one we specify : experiment with different sausages – garlic, smoked, those from various countries – and add spice to the simple sausage!*

## Sausage and Meatball Casserole

(serves 4–5)
Preparation time: about 15 min
Cooking time: about 20 min
Suitable for the freezer

*about 200g (7oz) meatballs (home-made or canned)*
*about 200g (7oz) cocktail sausages*
*2 large onions*
*2 carrots*
*2 stalks of celery*
*25g (1oz) butter or margarine*
*2 leeks, 1 clove of garlic*
*¼ cucumber*
*1 large can of tomatoes*
*½ × 15ml tbsp (½tbsp) soy sauce*
*salt, pepper, paprika*
*marjoram, basil*

1 Sauté chopped onions, grated carrots and finely chopped celery in butter. Turn heat down, and add leek rings, crushed garlic and small cucumber cubes. Mix vegetables and stir.
2 Add peeled tomatoes, bring to boil and season to taste with soy, spices and fresh or dried herbs. Cover mixture and simmer for about 15 min.
3 Put the meatballs and cocktail sausages into the casserole with a little of the green top of the leeks (chopped up very finely). Cook in the sauce for about 5–10 min.
Serve piping hot with brown bread or sauté potatoes.

## Spiced Sausage Casserole

(serves 4)
Preparation time: 10–15 min
Cooking time: 15–20 min
Suitable for the freezer

*Left : Macaroni or noodles and buttered peas go well with Spiced Sausage Casserole.*

*4 large boiling sausages*
*4 onions*
*1–2 cloves of garlic*
*2 stalks of celery*
*25g (1oz) butter or margarine*
*1 large can of tomatoes*
*1 small can tomato purée*
*½–1 × 15ml tbsp (½–1tbsp) chilli sauce*
*salt, paprika*

1 Chop the onions, and place with crushed garlic and sliced celery in a pot with melted butter.
2 Sauté vegetables for a few min, add peeled tomatoes and tomato purée, bring to boil and simmer for about 10–15 min. (You can thicken the juices with 1 × 5ml tsp (1tsp) cornflour mixed with cold water if you like.) Season to taste with chilli sauce, but be careful, as it is strong. Add salt and paprika and heat the sliced sausages in the gravy.
Serve with macaroni or noodles and buttered peas.

## Smoked Sausage Casserole

(serves 4)
Preparation time: about 10 min
Cooking time: 10–15 min
Suitable for the freezer, but will lose some taste

*about 450g (1lb) boiling smoked sausage*
*250g (9oz) macaroni (short-cut)*
*8–10 shallots or small onions*
*25g (1oz) butter or margarine*
*1 × 5ml tsp (1tsp) curry powder*
*1 × 15ml tbsp (1tbsp) plain flour*
*salt, pepper*
*about 300ml (½pt) stock*
*100ml (4fl oz) double cream*
*mustard, chives*

1 Boil macaroni in lightly salted water and drain in colander.
2 Scald and peel onions, cut in four and brown lightly in butter. Turn heat down, and leave onions to cook until tender.
3 Sprinkle with curry powder and flour, leave to sauté for a while, then add stock. Cook and stir until smooth, then add sliced sausage, macaroni, double cream and mustard to taste. Heat casserole through thoroughly, and season to taste with salt and pepper. Sprinkle chopped chives on top.
Serve with bread and a mixed green salad.

## Smoked Sausages and Cabbage

(serves 4)
Preparation time: about 15 min
Cooking time: 25–30 min
Suitable for the freezer

*about 450g (1lb) smoked sausages*
*¼ white cabbage*
*25g (1oz) butter or margarine*
*300–400ml (½–¾pt) stock, salt*
*6–8 peppercorns*
*2 bay leaves*
*a little tarragon and thyme*
*French mustard*
*1 sprig of parsley*

1 Shred and chop cabbage and sauté in butter in a casserole on low heat. Add 2 × 5ml tsp (2tsp) salt, stock, with whole peppercorns, bay leaves and fresh herbs and spices tied in a little muslin bag. (Dried herbs can just be sprinkled over.)
2 Bring to the boil and simmer, covered, for about 15 min. Slice sausages and put into casserole. Season to taste with mustard and cook for a further 10 min. Sprinkle with finely chopped parsley.
Serve with rye bread and mustard.

## Chipolata Casserole

(serves 4)
Preparation time: about 10 min
Cooking time: 20–30 min
Suitable for the freezer

*450g (1lb) pork chipolatas (cooked or raw)*
*2 onions, 2 carrots*
*700g (1½lb) potatoes*
*2 sprigs of parsley*
*salt, pepper*
*1 bay leaf, a little thyme*
*about ½l (1pt) stock*

1 Wash and prepare vegetables and slice finely. Place them in layers in a casserole with salt, pepper, finely chopped parsley, crushed bay leaf , thyme, and stock to cover.
2 Cook vegetables until nearly tender, then place raw sausages in the casserole and add more stock if necessary. Leave sausages to simmer until ready. (Cooked sausages should be sliced and placed in casserole to heat thoroughly.)
3 Remove the cooked raw sausages, cut in chunky slices, and put back into casserole. Sprinkle with finely chopped parsley.
Serve with bread and mustard.

# Vegetable Stews

*In each of these stews, individual flavours of the vegetables are deliciously to the fore.*

## Leek Stew

(serves 4–5)
Preparation time: about 20 min
Cooking time: 1–1½ hr
Suitable for the freezer

*about 1kg (2¼lb) pork shoulder,
    boned*
*2 onions, 2 × 15ml tbsp (2tbsp) oil*
*salt, pepper, paprika*
*mustard, stock*
*3 carrots, 3 potatoes*
*Tabasco or chilli sauce*
*5–6 medium leeks*
*2 tomatoes, nutmeg, chives*

1 Brown meat in the piece and chopped onions in oil and season with salt, pepper and paprika. Blend 1–2 × 5ml tsp (1–2tsp) mustard with about 400ml (¾pt) stock and pour over meat in casserole. Cook over low heat, covered, for about 1 hr.
2 Wash, peel and slice carrots and potatoes, and place in casserole. Add more water to barely cover contents (if necessary) and simmer for 20 min. Remove meat and cut into small chunks. Return to casserole. Season meat juices to taste with Tabasco or chilli sauce.
3 Slice leeks into 4–5 cm (1½–2in) thick pieces, keeping as much of the green as possible. Place leek in casserole with peeled, quartered tomatoes, and cook till everything is tender. Season to taste with grated nutmeg, finely chopped chives, salt and pepper.
Serve with brown rye bread and mustard.

## Spinach Stew

(serves 4)
Preparation time: about 10 min
Cooking time: about 15 min
Suitable for the freezer, but will lose some taste

*1 cauliflower, salt, pepper*
*300–400ml (½–¾pt) milk*
*15g (½oz) butter or margarine*
*450g (1lb) fresh spinach or 1 large
    packet frozen*

*1 × 15ml tbsp (1tbsp) cornflour*
*100ml (4fl oz) double cream*
*2–3 × 15ml tbsp (2–3tbsp) grated
    cheese, nutmeg*
*left-over cooked, smoked meat or
    sausages*

1 Divide cauliflower into flowerets, rinse well and simmer until nearly tender in seasoned milk.
2 Rinse fresh spinach (or thaw frozen) and steam for about 4 min in butter. Place in casserole with cauliflower and add strips of meat or sausage chunks.
Mix flour with the cream, and stir carefully into casserole. Add salt, pepper and grated nutmeg to taste. Remove casserole from heat and stir in grated cheese. Hot toasted cheese goes well with this stew.

## Pea Stew

(serves 4)
Preparation time: about 20 min
Cooking time: about 1½ hr
Not suitable for the freezer

*about 1kg (2¼lb) lamb for stewing
    (shoulder or neck cuts)*
*salt, black peppercorns*
*1 clove of garlic, 4 small carrots*
*2 onions*
*25g (1oz) butter or margarine*
*400g (14oz) frozen peas*
*1 × 15ml tbsp (1tbsp) plain flour*
*200ml (7fl oz) double cream*
*250g (9oz) mushrooms*
*1 lemon*
*1 sprig of parsley*

1 Place meat in cold water with 1 onion, garlic, carrots, 6 peppercorns

*Left : Leek Stew. You can use gammon instead of the pork which gives it a smokier taste.*

*Right : Beef and green beans combine well in Green Bean Stew.*

and 2–3 stems of parsley. Water must only just cover meat. Bring to boil and skim well. Add 1 × 5ml tsp (1tsp) salt, cover and simmer on low heat until meat is tender.
2 Remove meat, remove bones and slice. Sieve stock and slice boiled carrots and onion.
3 Sauté 1 chopped onion in $\frac{1}{2}$ the butter and add defrosted peas and stock. Leave vegetables to simmer for about 6–8 min and meanwhile brown cleaned mushrooms in remaining butter. Season to taste with salt and lemon juice.
4 Mix double cream and flour together and stir into the boiling vegetable stew. Add meat, carrots, onion and mushrooms, season gravy to taste with more spices and sprinkle with chopped parsley and finely grated lemon rind.
Serve with boiled potatoes.

**Green Bean Stew**
(serves 4–6)
Preparation time: about 20 min
Cooking time: about 2 hr
Suitable for the freezer

*700–900g ( 1½–2lb) slightly salted beef (brisket)*
*2 onions, peppercorns*
*4–5 small carrots*
*4 potatoes*
*1 sprig of rosemary*
*450g ( 1lb) green beans*
*50–100g (2–4oz) cream cheese.*

1 Bring beef to the boil in unsalted water and skim well. Add chopped onions, 10 black peppercorns and fresh or dried rosemary, and simmer on low heat, covered, until meat is tender. Remove meat and cut into small cubes.
2 Sieve stock. Wash and peel carrots and potatoes, slice, and boil until nearly tender in stock. Add stringed, chopped green beans and meat and leave to simmer for about 10 min. Mix cheese with some of the warm stock to a smooth cream and stir into stew. Season to taste with salt.
Serve hot with brown bread.

**Onion Stew**
(serves 4–6)
Preparation time: about 15 min
Cooking time: about 40 min
Suitable for the freezer before covering with cheese and browning

*100–200g (4–7oz) cooked ham*
*4–5 medium potatoes*
*¼ celeriac or 2 stalks of celery*
*6 large onions*
*2 thin leeks*
*25g (1oz) butter or margarine*
*1 bay leaf, 1 sprig of thyme*
*stock*
*200ml (7fl oz) single cream*
*salt, pepper*
*grated cheese, chives*

1 Wash and peel or scrape vege-

tables, and slice into cubes or strips. Sauté everything – except the green of the leeks – in butter on low heat for about 15 min.
2 Crush bay leaf and finely chop fresh thyme or crush $\frac{1}{2}$ × 5ml tsp (½tsp) dried. Sprinkle herbs over vegetables and add stock until contents are covered. Simmer for 25–30 min under lid.
3 Cut ham in strips and cook in casserole with the green part of the leek cut in thin rings for about 10 min. Stir in cream and season to taste with salt and pepper.
4 Sprinkle with grated cheese and place under hot grill until cheese is nice and golden. Garnish with chopped chives. Serve immediately with brown bread.

# Index